The Big Book of Whittling for Beginners

20 Easy and Fun Whittling Project Ideas and Design Patterns You Can Carve from Wood With Step by Step Wood Carving Instructions and Pictures

By

Luke Byrd

Disclaimer

This publication is designed to provide competent and reliable information regarding the subject matter covered. However, the views expressed in this publication are those of the author alone, and should not be taken as expert instruction or professional advice. The reader is responsible for his or her own actions.

The author hereby disclaims any responsibility or liability whatsoever that is incurred from the use or application of the contents of this publication by the purchaser or reader. The purchaser or reader is hereby responsible for his or her own actions.

Table of Contents

Introduction

If you are a lover of nature, then there is every possibility that you love trees.

What's there not to love?

A home for the birds in the cool of the evening. A warm shade for you from the scorching heat of the sun. A rendezvous point for friends and lovers to hang out and be one with nature. A safe haven from the heavy drops of the unexpected rain that pelts the skin of the person who walks through the park.

Another thing to love about trees is the fresh smell that comes from the woods in the cool of the day. Those smells can be refreshing and can be the reminder you need to take some time off from the bustle of life.

The fact that they play a major role in maintaining a healthy environment earns them brownie points in your book. Sadly, a time comes when these trees can no more stand and have to be cut down for other purposes.

Even in this state, they are useful. Furniture for houses. Timber for the fire to keep you warm in the cold of the winter, and many other uses of the wood from these trees.

Another use you may or may not have known is that the wood that comes from these trees are useful to you in artistic ways. With them, you can carve and create new projects to your heart's content. One of the easiest ways to manipulate wood without having to rely so much on heavy machinery is through the art of whittling.

Whittling can be considered to be the art of wood sculpture, on a simpler and less complicated scale. If you can master the art of whittling, you will see that there are many possibilities available for you.

In the pages that follow, we will be delving deep into the concept of whittling.

You will learn;

- What whittling is all about.
- The foundational terms you have to acquaint yourself with as a whittler.
- Whittling gear and their uses.
- A few whittling projects that you can embark upon, without a lot of prior knowledge and without a lot of machinery.

If you have ever harbored the thoughts of creating beautiful pieces out of wood, then you need to keep turning the pages.

Chapter 1

What is Whittling?

Whittling may refer either to the art of carving shapes out of raw wood using knife or a time-occupying, non-artistic process of repeatedly shaving slivers from a piece of wood. This process is used by many as a pastime or as a way to make artistic creations.

Simply put, whittling is the process of creating artworks from pieces of wood. The way artwork can be created from concrete by sculpting makes you think of whittling as sculpting wood. As mentioned earlier, many people have adopted it because of a lot of reasons, including the fact that the process can have therapeutic benefits and that it is a great pastime.

Whittling is a mid-level art. This implies that anyone can carry out this art - irrespective of your knowledge of the art and your skill level. Once you are equipped with the right knowledge, you have the time and patience required to create the projects you want to, and the materials needed are available, then there is no limit to what you can achieve with your whittling projects.

History of Whittling

Wood whittling is easily considered as one of the earliest methods of wood carving. It developed when a sharp stone was used to create a lovely piece from a piece of wood. From then on, people began to find more ways to make the job easier for them as it became apparent that there were more uses for wood than for fire and every other thing it was being used for when humans began to live on the planet.

Between the century 1865-1955, whittling was more prevalent in the United States. This was the time of the civil war. One of the effects of this war was that it caused many to be dislodged from where they lived. As lives began to be threatened, people had to relocate. This relocation pushed people farther away from civilization and developed areas of the country into more secluded areas. As is the way things are when there is a war, the spirits of men began to get dampened after a while and this was not needed if they were going to win the war.

To keep hope alive, men began to look for ways to get their minds off what was happening at the time and at least, have some amount of respite - even if it is for a few minutes every day. This forced the men who were alive and under these conditions to start gathering together in small groups at night. When they gathered, they lit fires and hung around these fires, telling stories that made their hearts merry, while carving away at the wood. For some, the carving on wood (whittling) was a mindless venture, and they saw it as an opportunity to enjoy themselves. These were the people who did not take it seriously. Although it is safe to assume that not a lot of people began this process with a desire to carve elaborate designs, some created designs that were considered beautiful at the time (not forgetting the fact that some of these were helpful to some extent, and not just to be kept as relics). These soldiers had one advantage that made whittling easy for them - the folding Jack knife they were given as soldiers. As is the manner of humans, they had found a use for the knives that were more than what they had thought in the first place.

As time went on, the art and craft began to evolve more. As some soldiers began to get exceedingly good with the art, they found the need to bequeath their knowledge to others. They did this mostly to children who had reached the age of understanding what they were doing, could follow instructions and be generally interested in knowing how to make the craft that was the pulse of the time. In addition to these, some adults did not mind learning from other adults the craft that was gradually becoming highly sought-after.

This was how things were until the war ended.

After the civil war, people began to return to their normal lives. As these men that had retreated began to return to the bustle of their urban lives, they were not returning as the people they once were. Many of them had gotten better with their whittling skills and as they returned to the cities and to their lives, they saw the need to take it a step further by teaching more children the skills they had gotten and seeing to it that these children became as good as they were, or even better. In search of a new balance and a means of livelihood, these men began to travel around the country, searching for work. At the time, the bulk of the available jobs were at railroads, lumbering, farming, and other physical jobs that required a lot but did not pay a lot at the end. Many of these soldiers had to pick up these jobs they would not have ordinarily done out of choices.

Because they were not getting enough, they still had to find a way to make more money. Those who had gotten good with whittling on the war grounds began to see that people were getting attracted to their artwork in strange lands. Many of these men resorted to selling their whittled art and using the monies for their upkeep as a sidekick. This was the beginning of the industrialization of whittling.

Ever since, whittling has come a long way.

Although not as popular now as it used to be a few decades and centuries back, you cannot negate the fact that whittling (if done well) is an amazing craft that you can use to produce creative projects to the limits of your imagination.

Since the 18th-century men began to sell and live off their whittled crafts, there have been many advancements in the art.

How Does Whittling Work?

First of, know that whittling is different from carving.

While both words tend to be used interchangeably (and justifiably so, considering that they both involve chunking at wood to get it to a particular shape), whittling is less demanding than carving. Usually, if you have the right kind of wood and a little knife that is sharp enough, you should be able to whittle. On the other hand, carving demands a lot more skill and specialized equipment to make it work.

Basically, here are the steps you will most likely go through if you want to get started on any whittling project. These steps should give you an idea of how the whittling exercise works and how you should carry it out;

A. Make sure you have the right materials for your project. We will cover the materials you need to have a successful project much later in this book. This knowledge is necessary to make sure that you do not waste your energ9ies on things that will not turn out to be as successful as they should be in the end.

B. If you are a beginner (which you most likely are reading this book), it is best to start with uncomplicated projects. It may not be the best thing for you to start whittling a dove, especially if that is your first project. There is every chance that notwithstanding the number of Youtube videos you see or guidebooks you read, you may end up making a mess of the project at hand. If you are big on safety, you should start out with a project as easy as whittling a wooden egg. This will help you with a lay of how the craft works and get you to feel everything you need to know to proceed to more complicated tasks.

C. Take it a step at a time. There is every tendency that after whittling the wooden egg, you may deem yourself fit to try your hands on something as complicated as trying to whittle a miniature Santa Claus. This is not the best idea for you because you may end up making a mess of the project, wasting your time, and harming yourself.

D. When whittling, be sure to put yourself in the emotional space where you are paying attention. This is not the kind of task you get done as proof that you are skilled in the art of multitasking. The ruined project or your bloody hands will testify that that was not the smartest move you could have made.

E. Follow the step by step procedures for the project that you want to work on. Trying to reinvent the wheel may not be in your best interest as you may not like what you will be left with. Some projects are discussed much later on, with a step by step guide. Follow these to the letter and you should have something you will be proud of.

F. Some tips and strategies are shared as well. These are shared to help you with your whittling projects and make sure that you have the best of experiences.

Health Benefits Of Whittling

A. Whittling is great because it allows you to relax your thoughts. This is one of the most apparent benefits of whittling. Seeing as it is a motor activity that requires complete concentration, it is a great exercise that allows you to zero in on the present and create whatever it is you are creating. Whittling helps you create a clear mind as you begin to process your thoughts more coherently. It is a mindful activity that can help you if you feel too stressed or burnt out.

B. Whittling can also help you with your emotions. Usually, people tend to bottle up their feelings and these feelings blow over to affect others around them - positively or negatively. Another way whittling can help you with mindfulness is that it allows you to let go of some steam. If you feel angry, frustrated, sad, happy, or any other thing in-between, whittling is a great way to let things go. Also, whittling allows you to express yourself without thinking of what people will have to say or not say about what you have created. These have a great effect because they can play a major role in reducing your stress levels and blood pressure.

C. Above all these, whittling has been shown to affect our spirit. This is most applicable to you if you believe in the spiritual aspect of life. Whittling connects you back to nature, and as a result of this, you begin to feel as though you are one with the universe at some point. Typically, when you are out in the fields on a day of clear weather, there is every tendency that you will feel good. There is no reason not to. The air smells different from that of a busy city; animals' sounds fill the air; you are alone with your thoughts.

Although not exactly the same, these things also tend to happen when you begin to whittle. When cutting into the wood and shaping something better out of it, deep connection tends to grow between yourself and nature. This fills you with a sense of calm and also of purpose. Also, the knowledge that you are creating another thing out of wood that was originally dead is an emotional/health/purpose booster that can mean the difference in many areas of your life.

Chapter 2

Basic Whittling Terminology

As a whittler, there are some words you cannot do away with. These are the terms you will come across while you carry out the craft. Here are a few of these terminologies;

Whittling

This is the process of creating amazing arts and crafts by shaping wood. It is similar to wood carving, but less demanding because almost anybody can carry out the task, and you do not need a lot of training to make it work.

Wood grain

Wood grain is the longitudinal arrangement of wood fibers or the patterns that result from this arrangement. It is necessary to understand this because the wood grain plays a major role in any whittling project's success. To have an easier project, you must first understand the wood grain because if you whittle in the same direction as the wood grain, it will be easier for your patterns to be formed on the wood than if you were to go against the wood grain.

Pocket knives

This is a kind of small knives that you can use to create whittling projects. For a long time, pocket knives were used for this craft because they were small and can fit into the palm of a grown man's hand easily, light and can be maneuvered easily, and usually sharp. Pocket knives (and by extension, all the knives that can be used for whittling) are the first things you should understand how they work because they play a major role in the success of any whittling projects(s).

Basswood

This is a type of wood that is known for being used for woodcarving. During the middle age, basswood was the preferred wood for German sculptors who embarked on more detailed projects. Because it does not have much grain and is exceedingly soft, it is the type of wood you want to look out for, especially as you get started with whittling.

Whittling cuts

To make the most of your whittling journey, you must know that several types of whittling cuts exist. This is the term used to describe how you must cut a piece of wood to get the desired shape or structure you want for it to have.

More on whittling cuts are discussed in a later section of this book.

Wood router

This is a hand-held or powered tool that hollows out an area in wood. They are mainly used in bigger woodworking forms as they save you the energy you would have lost trying to chip off the wood manually. If you do a lot of woodwork, or you know you will be engaging in heavy activities, you should try getting a wood router even before you get started.

Arkansas

This is a type of natural oil sharpening stone for achieving the final cut to a chisel's edge.

Bleaching

This is a process of treating the wood you want to whittle so that the surface looks lighter than it was and without unwanted marks or blemishes.

Dog

This is a metal clip with serrated ends that are used to clamp work that is being done to a bench.

Finishing

This is part of the final stages of whittling that most projects undergo. It is the stage that involves coloring, making the surface texture of the project even, sealing what you have carved out and waxing the project. Finishing is done to make sure that you do not turn out a terrible looking whittled projects. It does not have to be anything elaborate. What matters is that you put in some effort to make sure that the end product is neat enough to be desired by people who come across it.

Fuming

This is a method of adjusting the physical appearance of certain wood types. Fuming is the process of exposing wood to ammonia fumes and specific kinds of fumes to make the wood become darker and more suitable for what you want to whittle. Generally, this can be considered as the opposite of bleaching.

Incised work

This is the name given to any kind of work where designs are carved into the wood's surface, as opposed to projects where different pieces of wood are designed and joined together afterward. Incision is relatively easier than going the long route of designing and carving different wood pieces, then joining everything together in the end.

Chapter 3

Top Whittling Tips and Tricks

Here are a few tips and tricks you should have up your sleeves to get the best out of your whittling projects.

A. One of the first tips you will ever need for whittling is to choose the right tools for your project. Start by selecting the right knife to use, the right gloves or thumb pads to cover your hands with, and every other thing you will need for the project. Having the right tools is already half the work you will have to do if you will have a smooth sail.

B. Pay attention while whittling. There is every tendency that you will start up your projects with the right kind of knife and that it will be sharp. If you are on a project that involves a lot of work and that will take time, you will begin to notice that it will start getting increasingly difficult to get your knife through the wood after a time. At this point, you will have to spend more energy to push the knife through and get the shape you want to. There is every tendency that you may take this to mean that your limbs are getting tired.

While that could be the case, it may not always be like that. As a tip for making sure that your tools are at their best, stop whittling. Rather, take your knife over to the sharpening rod or anything you use to sharpen your knives and take some time to sharpen it. You may be surprised at what will happen once you resume your work with a sharp knife.

C. Before starting out on any project, take some time to understand the kind of wood you have available. The kind of wood at your disposal will determine a lot as it relates to the project you want to carry out. You cannot be working on a thick wood piece, and all you are trying to use is a little knife that is not as sharp. You will only get tired after a few tugs of the knife that will prove to be unfruitful. Also, you need to understand the wood grain structure. Whenever you whittle in the direction of the wood grain, your work will be easier and faster. If you go against the direction of the wood grain, you will have to pay a lot more in terms of the energy you will spend.

D. Do not let your children pick up the knife and begin to carve all by themselves, especially if they are still small and you haven't officially taken the time to teach them how to whittle. Children are hyperactive and would love to try out anything they see adults around them do. It is in the interest of the child's health and safety to make sure that this does not happen because their wounds may be too sore and/or too numerous.

E. Start small and grow into expertise. As you get started with whittling, there is every tendency that you would be tempted to jump the gun and try to whittle something intricate at the first chance you get. In addition to the fact that there is every possibility that you won't be able to get the complex project you have started out on, you may also end up wounding yourself with the whittling knife. It takes an exact skill that is developed to handle the knife. The more complex the project you are working on, the more you will need to be careful and know how to handle the materials you need carefully. To be on the safe side, begin whittling with small and simple projects (like the egg that was indicated above), and grow your way into making anything you would want to make.

F. Depending on how much of a people person you are, it is usually advisable that you whittle with the people you love and feel comfortable around. This is more advisable if you are embracing whittling as a relaxation task. They will help make you feel relaxed enough so that you do not try to rush through what you are doing, and their presence will help you concentrate on the success of the project at hand. This is one of the tips that every beginner whittler gets as he progresses with his journey in the craft.

G. To keep your hands free and not have to deal with the after effects of getting wounded during your project, you may want to consider keeping your hands free. Use a holding device like a clamp or vice to affix the wood you are whittling to a solid surface like a bench. This way, you can concentrate on whittling and not have to fear whether the knife will go the wrong way and tear away a part of your skin.

H. Give yourself time. Do not expect to be exceedingly good at whittling overnight. You have to give yourself the time and space to grow and get better with it.

Whittling requires patience and a lot of time. You will not create amazing projects if you lack these.

I. If you get a sliver in the wood when whittling, there is no need to be alarmed as long as all you have is a sliver. To get this off, place a piece of duct tape over where you have the sliver and gently pull the tape off after a while. This will take off the sliver and leave you with what you intended in the first place.

J. If you notice that you have selected the wrong type of wood and as a result, you are having difficulties trying to get the exact kind of detail you need in your whittling project, do not panic as there is a way around it. If your wood is either too hard or too soft, try getting it to what you need by applying a 50/50 mix of alcohol and water to the piece of wood by rubbing. This should help with the texture of the wood and make whittling easier for you.

K. If you are right-handed and working on a project that requires you to carve eyes on it, here's the best way to go about doing that. Complete the carving's right eye first (which is the left eye facing you). This way, you can see the eye exactly as it is while you work on it. When working in this progression, it is easier for you to spot out errors and make adjustments than it would have been if you were right-handed and you started out with trying to carve a left eye. When you are now done, you can go ahead to work on the left eye.

Reverse this procedure if you are left-handed and go for the left eye first.

A Short message from the Author:

Hey, I hope you are enjoying the book? I would love to hear your thoughts!

Many readers do not know how hard reviews are to come by and how much they help an author.

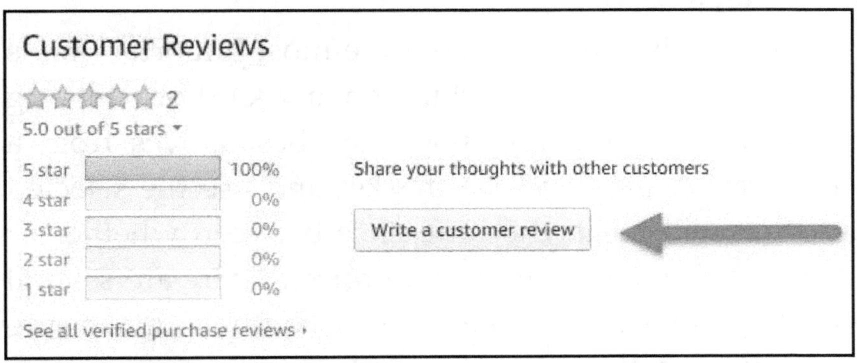

I would be incredibly grateful if you could take just 60 seconds to write a short review on Amazon, even if it is a few sentences!

>> Click here to leave a quick review

Thanks for the time taken to share your thoughts!

Chapter 4

Getting Started with Whittling

Basic Carving Supplies You Will Need

Whittling knives

Whittling knives are arguably the most important tools you need if you are embarking on any kind of whittling projects. Your ability to select the best knives from a vast array available in the market and use the selected one well will mean the difference between whether or not you will have a successful project. There are several whittling knives in the market and you must make sure that you select the one that is the best fit for your needs.

Before swiping your card out of your wallet and paying for any whittling knife, you should pay close attention to a few things. Since this is one of the tools that you will be using a lot, you mustn't skip these things. Here are a few of the things you need to consider so that you can be able to make the best decisions when it comes to the whittling knife you will use for your projects.

Things to consider before getting any whittling knife;

A. Type of blade

The type of blade is the first thing you must look at before getting any whittling knife. While stainless steel blades offer you the advantages of being cheaper, readily available online, and tending to be lighter, there is one major challenge with stainless steel blades; they tend to get dull quickly.

If you are looking to get a knife that you will still be using a few years later and many projects afterward, you should go for a knife that its blade is made of high-carbon steel. These blades take less to get sharpened and they take more time to wear or dull out when you use them. Also, these blades are tougher in that they can withstand more strain and do not tend to cave easily, even when they are subjected to a lot of stress by the user.

However, you may still want to go for the stainless steel blades if you are for convenience. Also, if you do not mind having to suspend your project frequently to go and sharpen your knives once and again, you can give them a trial.

B. Number of blades

Some more recent knives are made with the knowledge that the end-user of the knife will, at some point, have various needs and will have to make use of different knives. As a result of this, these knives usually come in packs, and most of these packs have up to 20 blades in them.

The major advantage of this is that these multi-blades give you the luxury of working on many projects without being afraid that you will soon get to a point where the blades will no more be able to cut through the wood you are whittling. Considering this, it is wise and resourceful to go for knives with three blades. This way, you have more options, and with more options, you save money while still achieving all that you want to achieve with one knife.

Also, there is a reason for three blades. If you go for a knife with 20 blades, the sheer number of blades in the knife will negatively affect your carving abilities. It will weaken your carving power and you may end up spending more time/energy trying to make sure that your fingers do not get in the way of any blades than the energy needed to carve the wood.

C. Locking blades

This is one of the first things you should consider before you get a whittling knife. Whittling knives that have locking blades should be on your to-buy list. This is because, with these knives, your safety is more assured.

One of the basic rules of whittling is that your safety comes first. A knife that has locking blades is safer for you because you have a way to put away the sharp blades and reduce your chances of getting hurt.

Here are a few whittling knives available for you;

A. Flexcut JKN88 Whittling Jack

This is a light knife that is a good bet for beginners to whittling. It is small enough to fit into the palm of a grown man, light enough not to be a burden and comes with the perfect shape to the blade that allows you to make the most precise cuts with as little as a few strokes.

This knife is easy to sharpen and takes a relatively long amount of time for it to lose out on its sharpness. This knife is obtainable at any online store.

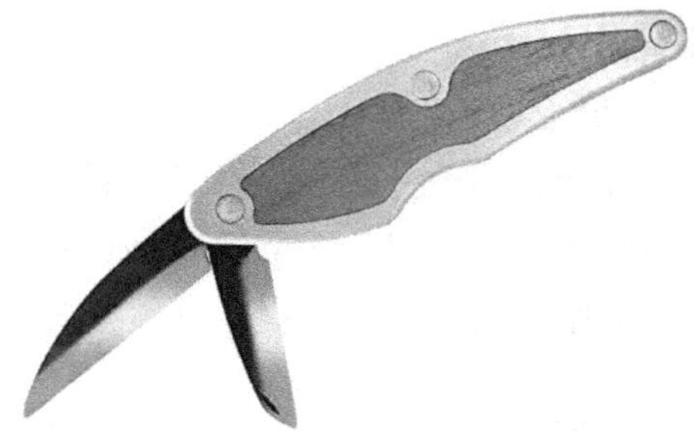

B. Flexcut detail knife

This is a very small knife that is most suitable for beginners. It has a framework that is simple, light and easy-to-use. With a pointed and sharp blade, this knife is a great option for you if you are looking to make simple designs and you will be punching or trying to create holes in the wood as you whittle.

This knife's strongest point is that its minimalistic design allows you to hold it for extended periods without feeling an ache in your hands. Also, its handle is made with comfort in mind.

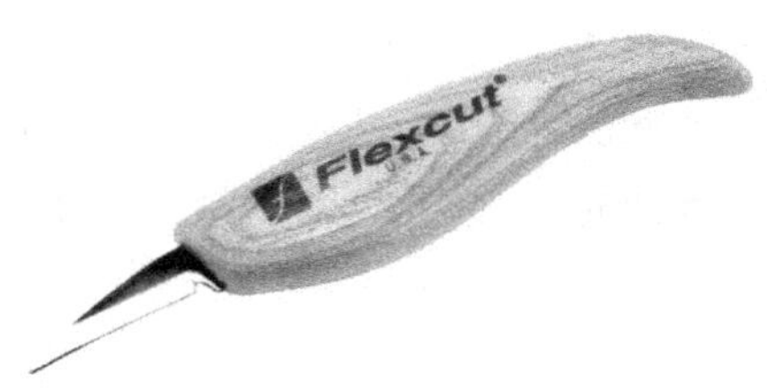

C. Morakniv Brand knives

There are many knives under this umbrella brand and all of them have their benefits as well. For example, the Morakniv 106 is well acclaimed for its pointed blade of laminated steel. This one feature makes it a go-to choice because of its strength, and edge resiliency. Because of these two features, it is a great knife for carving strong wood.

On the other hand, the Morakniv 120 is a smaller knife and this one feature makes it the best bet when you are looking to create something more intricate. This knife's handle is unique in that the center of the handle is thick, while it thins out on either side. As a result of this, the knife is a better option for you to consider if you are looking for something that will be comfortable if you will be whittling for long hours on projects that are of intricate designs.

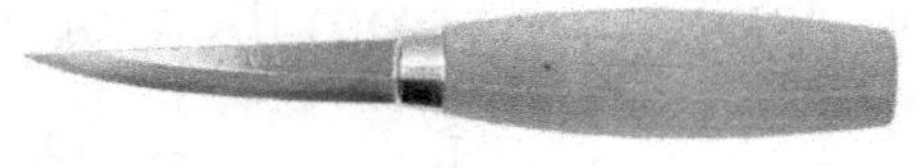

Morakniv 106

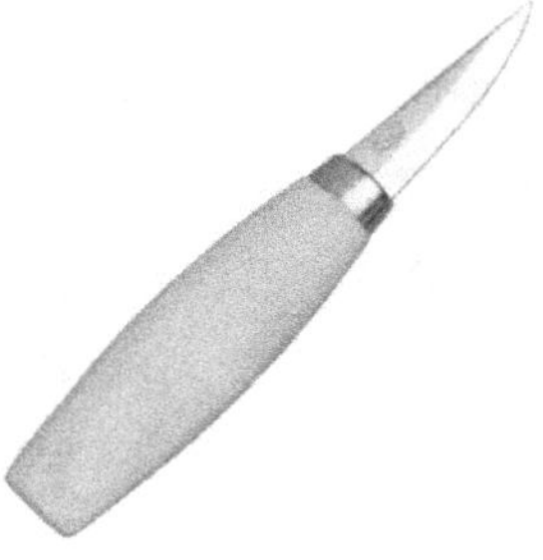

Morakniv 120

Whittling gloves

Whittling is an exercise that uses sharp tools. Choosing to protect yourself should be a no-brainer because if you decide to brave it out and start whittling without making the required arrangements to make sure that you are protected, you may end up hurting yourself. If this happens to you, you may be unable to whittle for a while until you have healed from the wound.

Many times, newbie whittlers refuse to wear gloves when they whittle. In their defence, the gloves make them feel uncomfortable. But when weighed against each other, what can happen to you if you wear gloves is better than what can happen if you refuse to. Under the best-case scenario, whittling gloves can get in your way and make you feel a bit uncomfortable. On the other hand, you can suffer a bad wound if you refuse to wear the right whittling glove, and you may even suffer a wound that may be irreparable.

So, the best idea will be to select the most appropriate hand covering material and be sure to be careful when you are about to whittle.

Generally, whittling gloves are worn on the hand that supports the wood you are carving. As a result, if you wear a glove on the hand that holds the knife without protecting the hand supporting the wood you are carving, you would have made a costly mistake because that in itself is a counter-productive measure.

There are several whittling gloves available in the market. It is left for you to breeze through and make the best choice for yourself, based on your needs.

Here are a few of them;

A. NoCry resistant gloves

These gloves are tough and are made of durable material. The silicon dots that cover the surface of these gloves makes them great at gripping awkward objects and as a result, offers you a better chance to do a better work of whittling. Despite these gloves' strength, they allow some air to enter your hands so that you do not begin to sweat through your palms and get uncomfortable.

If you use this glove well, you will see that injuries from your knife will be few and far between. This is because it offers the highest level of protection available in the market today. It can prevent cuts, tears, wounds from sharp edges, blades, etc.

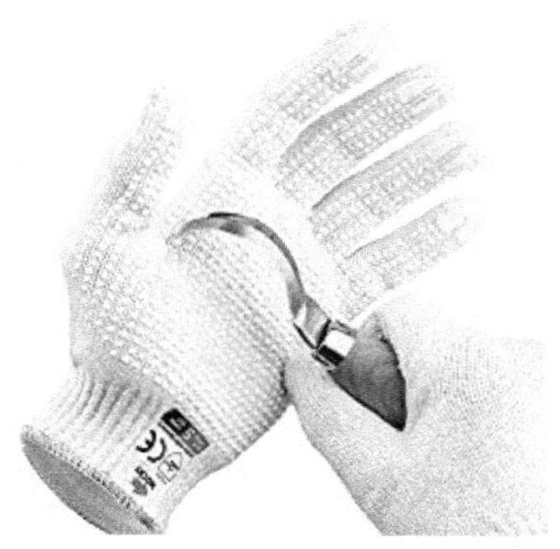

B. DEX Fit Durable Power Grip

This is another widely acclaimed whittling glove in the market. It comes with a lot of features that make it great for use. Some of these features include;

The ability to protect against cuts and punctures, a premium elastic knit wrist cuff for easy usability, and these gloves are built for diverse kinds of whittling. The nitrile coating on these gloves' palms makes them the best option for use if you are looking for something that allows you to have a firm grip on your wood as you whittle. You can purchase these gloves from any online store.

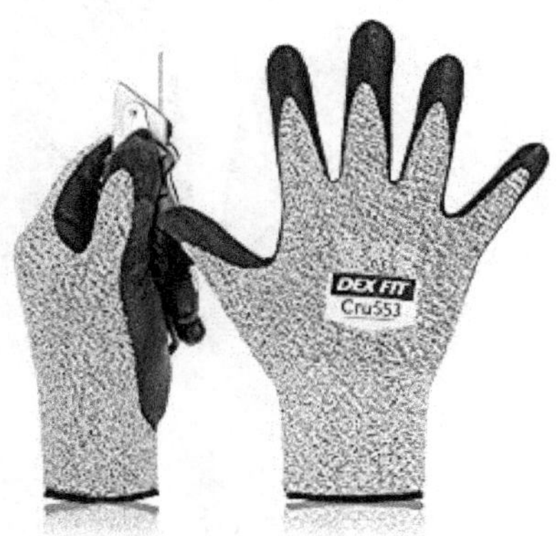

C. G & F Kevlar Knit gloves

This is another type of gloves that you need to have if you want to make the most of your whittling experience and not have to part with a nail or finger while at it. This is a strong glove with PVC dots that enhance the gripping experience. These dots are spaced out well and even as they provide the grip power, they also allow enough air to slip into your palms while you work so that you do not get sweaty hands.

This glove offers the perfect amount of resistance against slicing, tearing and wearing that comes from dealing with a lot of whittling projects. Like the others, you can purchase them from any online store.

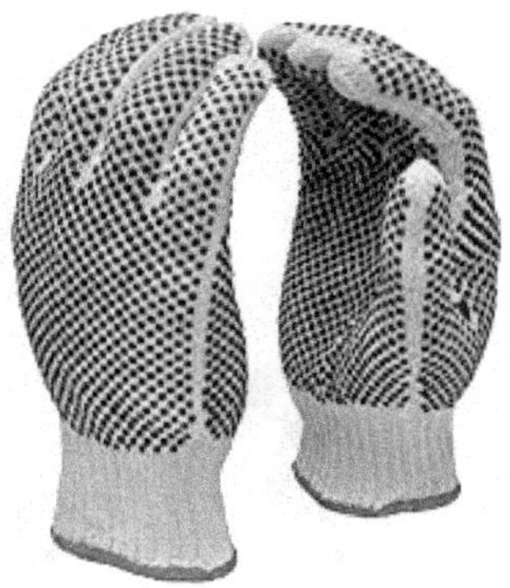

There are still a number of whittling gloves you can check out and make your choice from.

Wood

This is another material you will need for your projects. As a matter of fact, it is as important as every other tool that has been discussed above because, without wood, there won't be any whittling project in the first place.

There are a lot of wood types available for you, and all of them have their peculiarities. It is vital you know all these to know which wood to select for any of the projects you want to get started with. Here are a few of these wood types.

A. Basswood

This is the most commonly used type of wood for whittling. It is the most commonly used for whittling because of some of the characteristics it possesses, which include;

I. Its shiny and light-colored nature that makes it easy to be used for whittling.
II. Its softness and easily distinguishable wood grain pattern. These characteristics make basswood easy to be carved.

When allowed to choose, the average whittler will most likely go for basswood because of these characteristics that have been outlined above. Also, it does not require a lot of finishing when you are done with the projects.

B. Balsa wood
This is also a common type of wood used for whittling. A few things make it desirable for the purpose and they include;

I. Its availability in the marketplace and the fact that it is cheaper than other types of wood.
II. It is one of the softest woods available to whittlers in the marketplace.
III. It is highly pliable. This is because it is a soft type of wood. As a result of this, it can be used for precut wood models of heavier projects to be embarked upon like automobiles, boats, etc.

C. <u>Pinewood</u>
This is also another common type of wood available for whittling. One of the major advantages of this wood is that it is not hard to find. Pine is ubiquitous and grows across America. If you stay in a place with a lot of nature around it, you may not even have to go to a store to look for pine and even if you do, it most likely would be cheap.

Asides from this major advantage of availability, pinewood has some disadvantages associated with it. Because it is known to dry out easily, this wood cannot hold detail for a long time, and if you are carving something that requires you to make a lot of intricate details on it, pinewood may not be the best option for you. When fresh, pinewood can be used for anything, but your project may begin to lose detail as time progresses.

On the other hand, the fresh pinewood smell is a delight to a lot of people. This is another thing that earns this wood brownie points for a lot of people. This smell is released as you cut into the wood while whittling. On the downside, there is the pine sap that comes out while you whittle. It can be a nuisance, especially if you are new to whittling. In any case, pinewood is one you may want to give a try as you venture into whittling.

Whittling Knife Safety Rules

After selecting the whittling knife, you should stick to some rules to ensure that you get the most out of your whittling exercises and keep from hurting yourself.

Here are some of the top safety rules to abide by;

A. Be sure to use a whittling glove as you embark upon projects. This glove should be worn on the hand while holding the wood being whittled, or the idea of protecting the hand would have been defeated.

B. Return your knife to its blade lock when you are not using the knife. This helps make sure that people do not sustain cuts by mistakenly handling knives that are unsheathed.

C. Never treat your knife like it is a toy. Do not

I. Throw it at people for any reason.
II. Hand the knife over to people with the blade first.
III. Carry an open knife when you are interacting with people. If you must interact with people, take a few seconds to sheath it before getting on with what you want to do.

D. Do not try to cut with a dirty or blunt blade.

E. When cutting, never make cut toward your body. As a rule of thumb, cut away from your body. This makes sure that you do not make the mistake of cutting yourself with the knife as you whittle.

F. Maintain your pocket knife by keeping it clean and sharp. To clean, make use of a toothpick or something that you can use to poke dirt out of crevices that they may hide. Also, make it a point of duty to sharpen your knife as frequently as needed.

Choosing a Whittling Knife

This is an important part of the whole process. You must be sure that whatever knife you choose is suitable for the project at hand.

A number of characteristics were discussed in an earlier section. They are the characteristics a knife must have before you buy it for whittling. Refer to the section of the book and keep track of those characteristics.

Whittling Knife Basic Cuts

As you get ready to start with whittling, it is vital that you know the kinds of cuts you can make with your whittling knife. Here is a list of all the cuts you may make as you whittle;

A. Straightaway rough cutting

This is one of the primary cutting patterns used in whittling. It is mostly used to get the basic outline of the project ready. In this kind of cutting, you make long and sweeping cuts in the grains' direction that go away from your body. For the best effects, take this step gradually and resist the urge to get too deep while at it. This is what this kind of cut looks like;

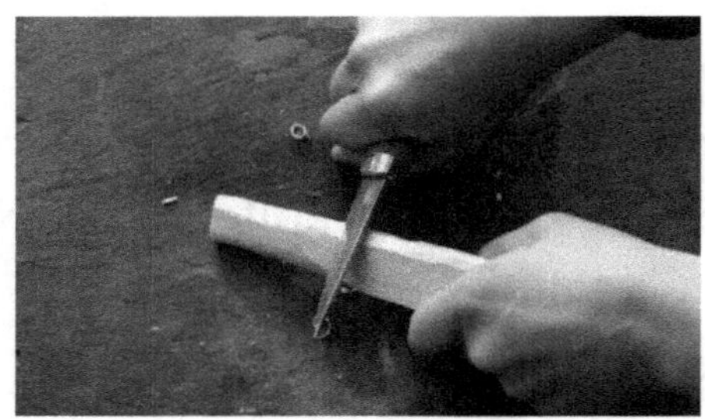

B. Thumb push stroke

This is used when you need to start making deeper cuts and shaping your project the more. It is done in the same way the straightaway rough cutting is done, but the non-cutting hand's thumb is used to provide the force needed to push the knife through the wood. All you need to do is place the thumb of your non-cutting hand on top of your blade and push into the wood in the direction you want the knife to cut.

Here's what I mean;

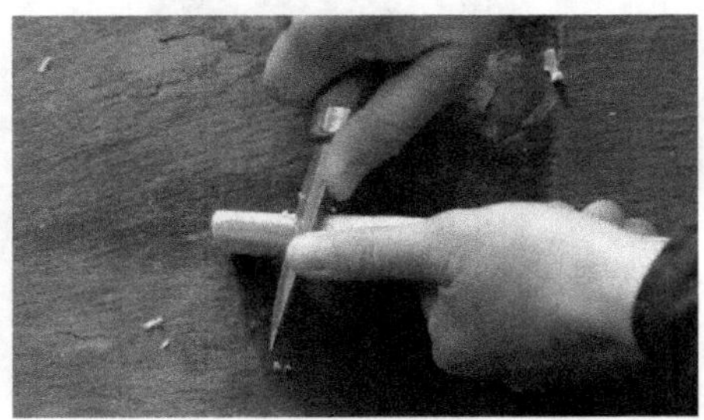

C. The Paring cut

Also known as the pull cut; the major difference between this stroke and the first stroke discussed is in the strokes' direction. To achieve this stroke, position the wood with the grains facing toward you. With a shallow and consistent stroke, cut the wood toward you. Be sure that while you do this, you have used your other hand to hold down the wood tightly, and also, be sure to protect the thumb of the hand holding the knife because in most cases, this thumb will be what will stop the knife from going too far off the piece of wood you are whittling.

This is what this stroke looks like;

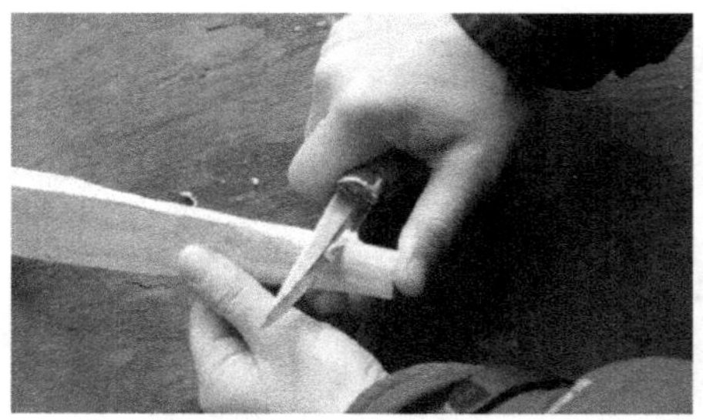

Basics of Whittling Knife Sharpening

As we have discussed earlier, it is vital for you to always work with a sharp knife. To make this work, you must know how to sharpen your whittling knife once the need arises. Here are the basics of whittling knife sharpening

A. Make sure that you always have a sharpening stone, sandpaper, and some leather in your whittling toolkit to make the most of your efforts and projects.

B. Invest in getting a good sharpening stone. The better your sharpening stone is, the easier it will be for you to work your way around projects. You do not have to break the bank to do this. There are a lot of great sharpening stones you can get for just a few bucks. You may want to take your time to make a great selection when you are ready to buy.

C. Sharpen your knife by trying out any of these methods;

I. Lay your knife at such an angle that it is close to being flat. Let the little projection from the flat surface be the knife's inclination on the sharpening stone. Drag the knife towards you as if you were trying to cut off a piece of the stone. Be sure that the knife's sharp edge is in contact with the stone as you do this repeatedly. After a while, your knife will start getting sharper. Know when it is sharp enough to cut through wood easily but not sharp enough to pass through the gloves on your hand and leave with a chunk of your skin.

II. Conversely, follow the same set up for the sharpening of your stone. Instead of dragging the knife towards you, push it away from yourself. This will also have the same effect as with option (I) above.

D. When you are done with the sharpening stone, you have to move on to stropping the knife. Stropping is the process of making sure that the knife you have sharpened has its edge hones so that it does not end up too sharp. To achieve this;

I. Get a piece of leather from your toolkit and spread some sharpening compound on it. One of the more common substances that can do in this context is Herb's Yellowstone.
II. Spread this sharpening compound evenly on the piece of leather you are to use for stropping.
III. Strop the knife by laying it as flat as you can on the piece of leather that has been coated and dragging the knife toward yourself while making sure that there are sufficient pressure and contact between the knife and the leather strop you are using. Do this until the knife looks less harmful than it was when you first brought it out of the sharpening phase.

Chapter 5

Whittling Project Ideas

Here are a few projects you can embark upon, even if you are a beginner in the art of whittling.

Wooden Egg

Supplies needed

- A piece of scrap wood (basswood or any soft kind of wood so that it can be easier for you). usually, go for one that measures 1.5 x 1.5 x 2. this should be easy on you.
- Your whittling knife
- Whittling gloves.
- Pencil

Steps

1. Find the piece of wood you want to use and make sure that you have laid out all the materials you need for the work.

1. Cut the wood so that the length and breadth are the same, and the depth is a bit longer than the other sides. For the best of results, let the depth be 1.3 times longer than the width (width × 1.3). The carved-out block will look like this.

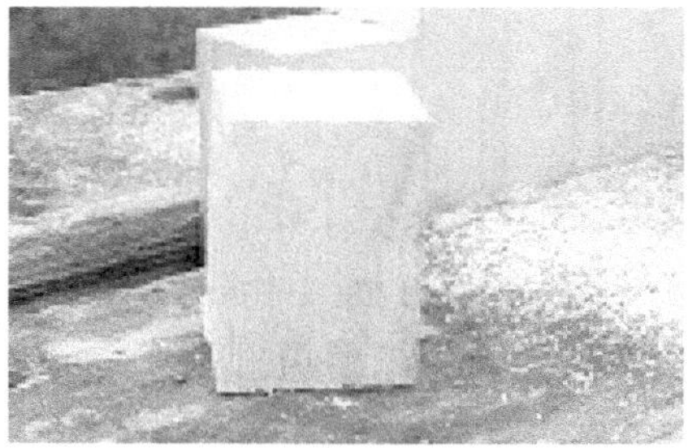

2. Carve both ends of the wooden piece you have cut out into rounds. Be very careful and be sure to make use of the push stroke or the thumb push stroke as you deem fit. After doing this, cut the edges away so that you are left with a cylinder.

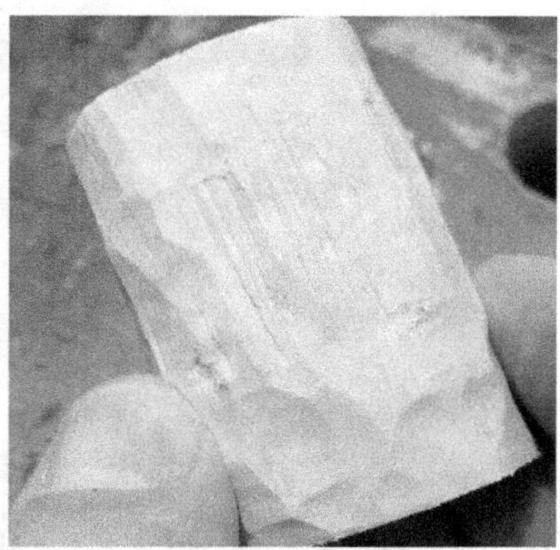

3. With a pencil, make a mark around the cylinder. This will be the widest point of the egg and you do not need to measure this. All you need is to do what feels right to you, so make a hands free measurement.

4. From the widest point you determined earlier, begin to carve both sides in. Be sure to incline the carving well, but do not touch the widest point you marked with a pencil.

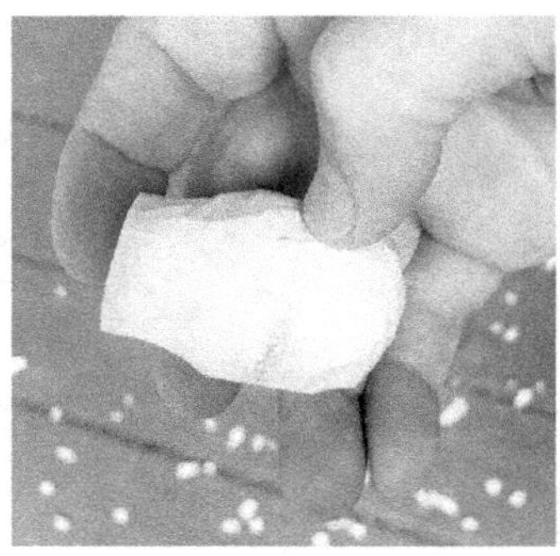

5. Make one end of what you are carving a bit pointy and to incline inward than the other end. This is going to be the top of the egg. For the other end, make it a bit less pointed than the first end. When you are done, you should have something that looks like this below.

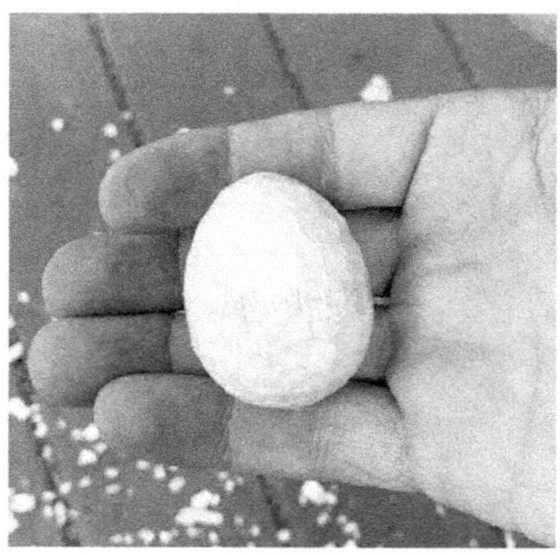

6. When you are done, you can choose to leave the egg as it is. But to make it more even, rub all over the egg

with sandpaper, and if you want to, apply some finish to it (oil, stain, paint, etc).

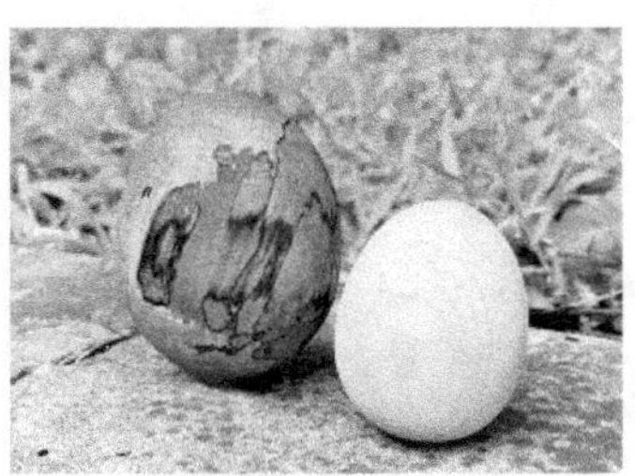

Miniature Bow and Arrow

This is a great project you can carry out on the spur of the moment, and you can do it with your child.

Supplies needed

- Craft sticks
- Dental floss
- Cotton swabs
- Whittling knives
- Scissors
- Cutting board

Steps

1. Lay out the stick you would like to use for your project on a flat surface, and with your knife, make a

cut of 2 1/16 to 1/8 inch slits side by side on one side of the stick. Let these cuts be near one end of the stick as shown below

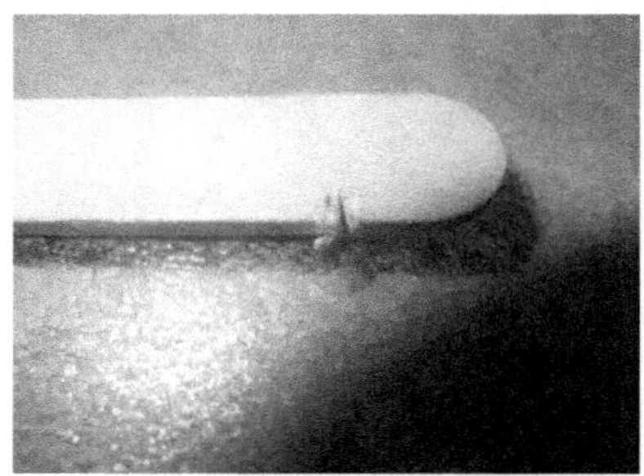

2. Repeat this for both sides of the same end of the stick. After doing this, clean out the marks you have made so you will be left with a hole on the stick's two sides. Repeat the entire process for the other end of the stick. At the end of this step, you should have two slits across from each other – on the two sides of the stick you are using.

3. Soak this stick for about 1 hour in a bowl of water. The goal of this is to allow it to soak in some water and get more malleable as the case may be.

4. Cut off more than 12 inches of dental floss (or just enough floss that will do for the size of the stick you

are using). The floss will be tied to the ends of the bow and serve as the bow's string. After doing this, tie a slip knot at one end of the floss you have cut out. Slip this knot into the slits you have on one end of the stick you are using for your bow. Be sure to wrap the floss around the slits so that it is firm enough, and secure the knots well. It should look this way.

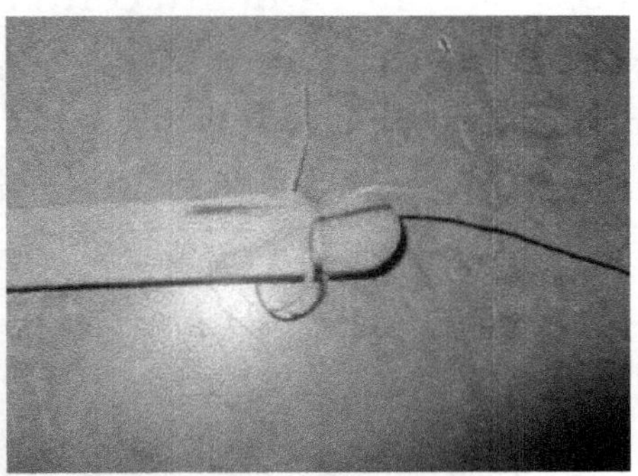

5. Gently bend the stick into a bow shape and tie the knot on the other side of the stick. Be sure to bend the stick carefully so it does not snap in two. Cut off the extra floss at the ends of the knots you have tied and allow the bow to dry.

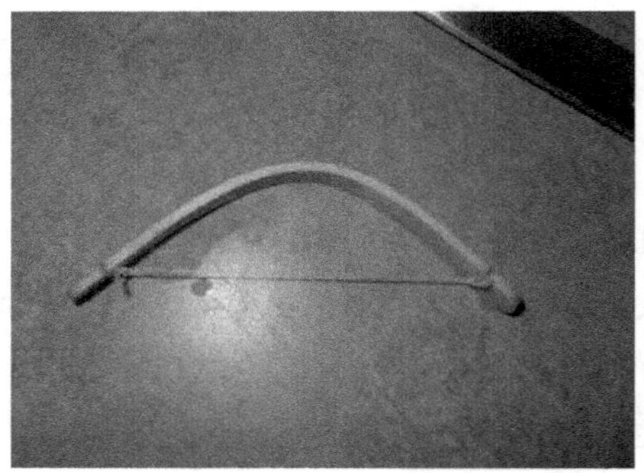

6. The easiest way to get your arrows is to make use of cotton swabs. Get out as many cotton swabs as you would like to use and cut one end of the swabs away. You now have arrows to go with your bow. Feel free to make as many as you would need.

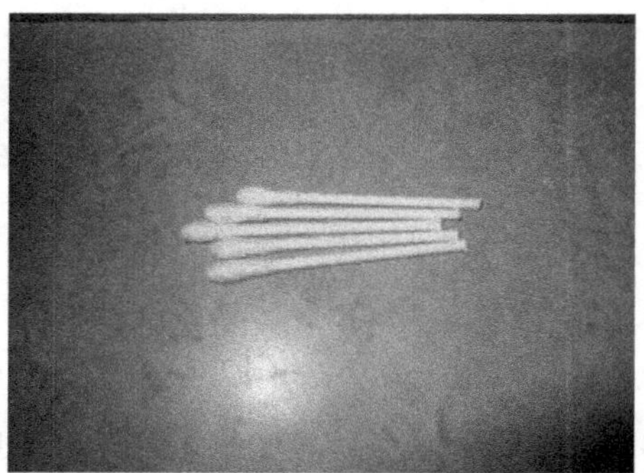

Willow Whistle

This is another easy project that you can complete in little to no time.

Supplies needed

- Willow stick
- Whittling knife

Steps

1. Get a willow branch that has its green bark. Arguably, many other wood types will work, but the aim of using willow is that you need something that you can slip its bark out of the wood without damaging the bark. This is what makes willow most preferable for the project at hand.

2. Cut a notch in the stick. This notch has to run across the stick, at about an inch or so from the end. Make the cut shallow and V-shaped. It should just be deep enough to get through the bark, but not too deep to cut far into the wood beneath the bark.

3. After cutting the notch, move back another inch and a half from the notch and cut a ring in the bark of the stick you are working on. After doing this, remove the bark as carefully as possible, so it comes out in one piece. To be on the safe side, you may want to start by tapping lightly on the bark to loosen it up a bit.

4. When the bark has gone off, carve the notch you created earlier to get deeper into the stick. For the best of results, carve deep and make sure that you extend the notch to get to the center of the stick. This hole should be at least 1/2 to 1 inch wide when you are done carving and cleaning it out. Also, create a flat plane in front of the hole you just burrowed. This is what the whistle should look like at this point.

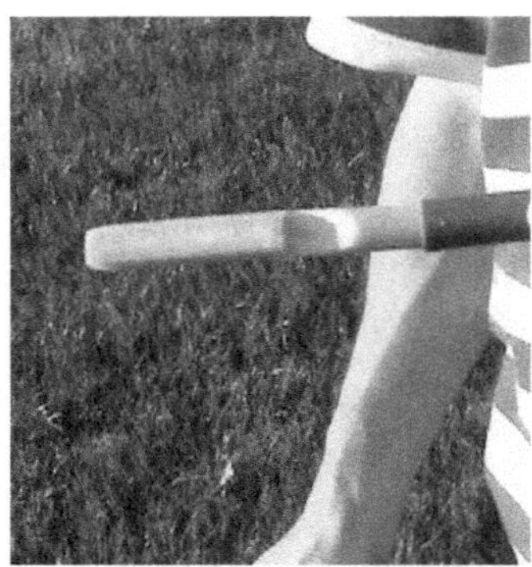

5. Cover the whistle once again with the bark you took off at first. This is why you have to pay attention to the way you handle the bark of the wood. You are going to slip it in once again. Hence, you need to make sure that you handle it with extreme care. Your whistle is done. To blow it, all you need to do is blow into the part of the bark you just replaced in the last step and it should be working as well as it should.

Spike Trolls

You can think of embarking upon this project if you are a parent or you have children around. This is because while it is fun and easy to work on, it is also a delight for children; both during and after the creation process.

Supplies needed

- Whittling knife
- Wood (basswood most preferable)
- Whittling gloves and other protective gear.

Steps

1. Cut out a piece of wood that you would want to make use of. Most preferably, let it be a cylindrical piece of wood that is as long as you would want your troll to be. Even if the wood piece you find is not a cylinder, you can carve it into that shape by carving out the excesses at the sides of the wood until you get it to a cylindrical shape.

2. When you have the wooden cylinder that is just about the size and height as you would want the spike troll to be, make a mark around the wood about halfway through it. This is where you will begin your work.

3. From the mark you made in the step above, begin to carve out excess wood toward the top of the piece you are working on. For your safety, you should use the pull stroke while doing this. The idea is to make the top end pointy, while the wood gets wider as it gets to the middle.

4. When you have the top part of the wood to be pointy, you may want to clean out what you have done with some sandpaper.

5. Whittle out a little bowl-shaped portion in front of the troll you are working on. This should start at the place where you marked round the wood, and project downward. In a nutshell, it should have a U shape.

6. Finish cleaning off the rest of the wood with sandpaper to ensure it is as smooth as it can be. Also, cut off a little part from the lower end of the wood so that you are left with a flat surface that you can set the troll on.

7. Experiment with designing and drawing a face on the troll you have created with some permanent marker of a distinguishable color against the piece of wood. This should do the trick for you. At the end, this is what the troll should look like

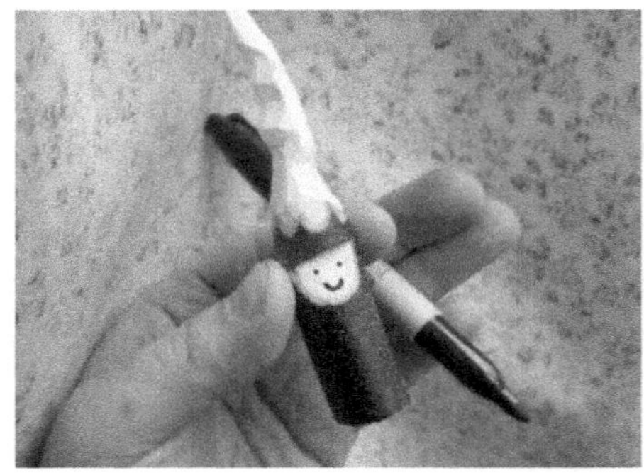

Small Wooden Valentine Hearts

This is the perfect, easy-to-make gift to give a loved one on valentine or any other day. It should not take more than a few minutes to complete, and that makes it perfect for you, even if you do not have the time to do something more elaborate.

Supplies needed

- Soft wood block like basswood block
- Carving knife
- Printing paper or cardboard paper
- Some paint or permanent marker, especially red-colored
- Sandpaper, and oil for finishing

Steps

1. Cut out a small-sized block from the printing paper you are making use of. The size of this block will be dependent on the size of the heart you want to produce, and the size of the wooden block you are making use of.

2. On the block of printing paper you have cut out, draw a heart the size you want it to be after you are done with the final project. Cut out the heart and do away with the excess paper.

3. Place this heart on the wood block you are working with and print the edges of the heart on the wood with the carving knife you have. This will create an outline of the heart on the wood block. You should have something like this

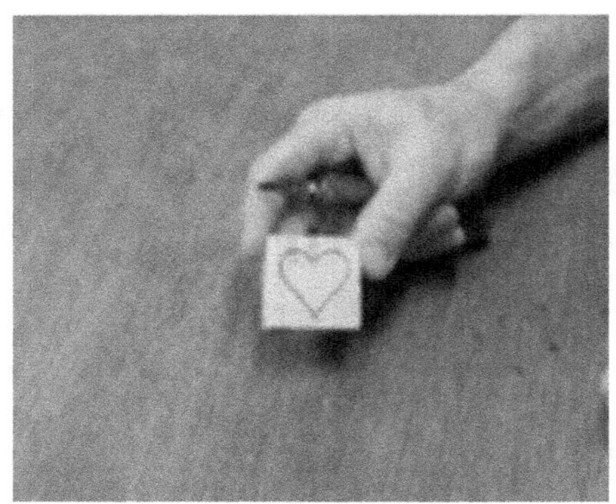

4. Carve down the edges of the wooden bar so that the heart is projected above it. After doing this, highlight the edges of your heart with the carving knife. This will ensure that it is clearly seen and that you do not make any mistakes with the project.

5. With your knife, make straight marks across the wooden block. However, make sure that those marks do not touch or run through the heart in the middle of the block. These will come out as grooves and add to the beauty of the project you are working on.

6. Go ahead to shape the edges of the wooden block and make sure that they are as smooth as they

can get. To make this much better, use a sandpaper to make sure that the edges are smooth.

7. Go ahead to paint the heart in the middle with the red color. Feel free to get creative with this step. The rules are not set in stone. You can paint whatever you feel will make the project look much better at this stage. Just remember that the idea is to make sure that you produce something which is beautiful. Here's what the final project will look like;

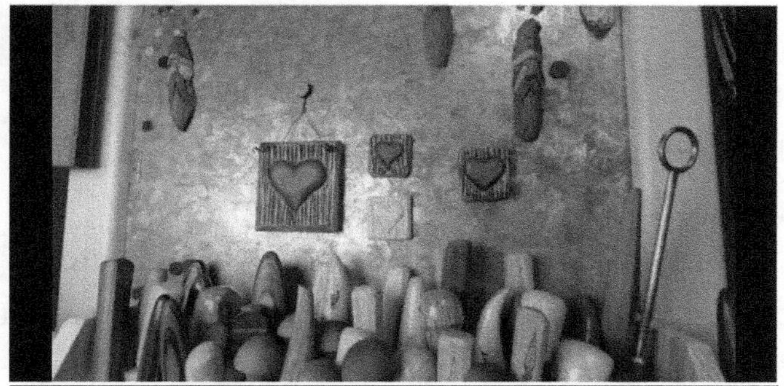

Wooden Spoon

This is one of the projects you can embark upon even as a beginner. Although you may need to pay some more attention to some details, if you can carry out this process well, you will see that the end will satisfy the efforts you have put in.

Supplies needed

- Carving knives
- A piece of soft wood. While selecting the wood you will use for your project, be sure that you are picking something a bit larger than the size of the spoon you want to carve.
- Sandpaper.
- Pen/marker
- Wood finish
- Saw.

Steps

1. Select the right wood for your project and lay it out on the work surface. Think of using wood that is softer to carve. As a beginner, you may want to stick with basswood.

2. On the wood bar you have selected, make an outline of the spoon you want to whittle. It does

not need to be too detailed. You only need this outline to create the framework for your spoon.

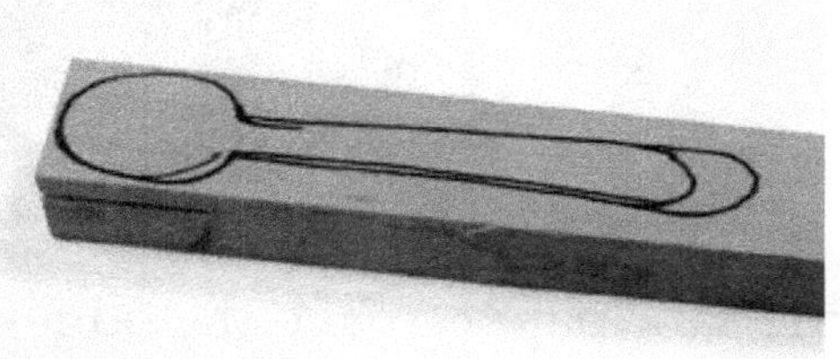

3. Cut out the spoon you have outlined on the wood blank. This should give you the first shape of the spoon you are working on. This is called the blank of wood you will make the spoon from.

4. With a scroll saw, cut along the outline of the spoon you have made. Try to make sure that you follow the outline as closely as you can so that you may reduce the amount of work you have to do as the project unfolds.

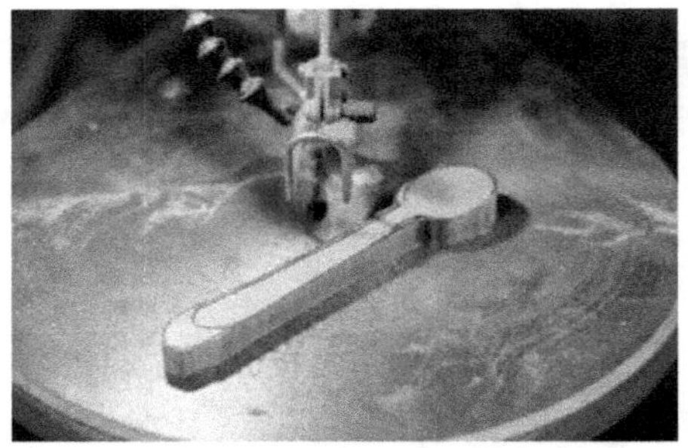

5. With the sandpaper, make the edges of the spoon smooth. This step is optional, but if you always look out for rough edges, you may want to get them out of the way.

6. After making the edges smooth, you want to add a few details to the spoon's handle. You can achieve this by carving out the sides of the center of the handle of your spoon. When you have done this on all four sides, make it smooth by using sandpaper. When you have added the details, you should have something of this nature;

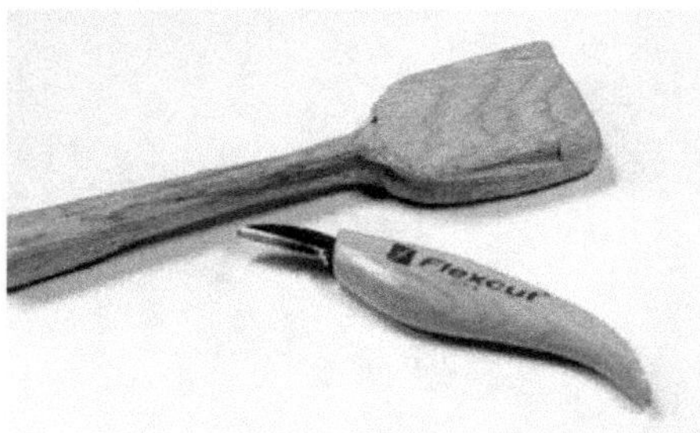

7. When you are done with the handle of the spoon, begin working on the back of the spoon head. Remove materials along the edge of the wood blank to make a smooth curve from the back of the handle to the rim of the wall of the wood.

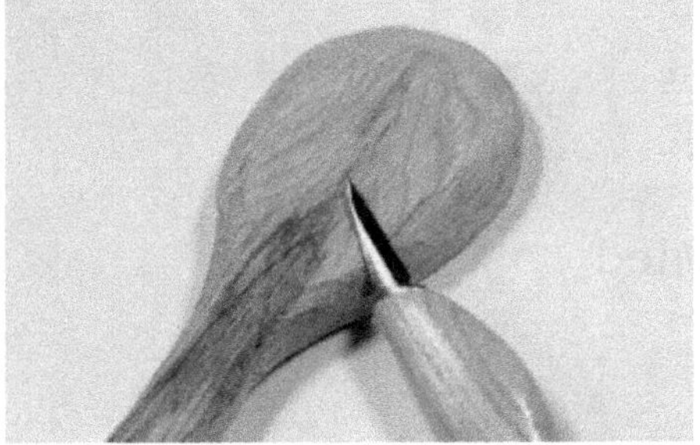

8. Work on the front of the spoon head and make a bowl in it. To achieve this, use a rounded sweep gouge or a hook knife to start removing material from the face of the spoon. Keep at this until you have formed a small bowl-like shape on the front surface of the spoon.

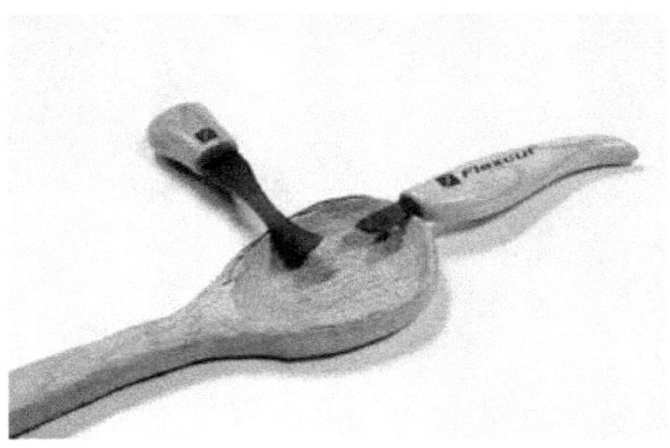

9. Put finishing touches to the spoon when you have achieved the shape you want it to be. Finishing touches include cleaning it up all around with sandpaper and using some oil finish to make sure that it is as clean as it can get.

Wooden Cups

Supplies needed

- Wood.
- Carving knife
- Protective gear
- Saw
- Sandpaper.
- Dremel

Steps

1. Get a round-shaped piece of wood. You can get this by looking for a piece of wood shaped this way or cutting it out of a wooden block available.

2. Rough shape the wood by sawing off any protrusions that are not useful to the teacup's final shape. While at it, make the length of the cup as semicircular as possible. This will be the final shape of the cup.

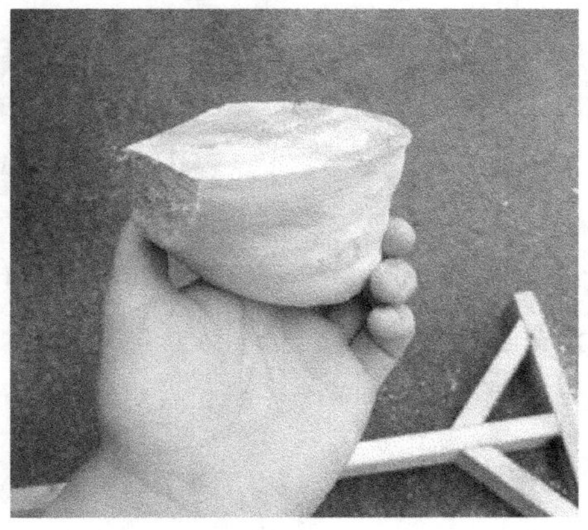

3. Shape the wood you have at this point with some sandpaper. If the cup has come out smooth till this point, you may want to skip this part. If the reverse is the case, please take some time to make this work.

4. At the top of the cup, draw a circle as large as you would want the cup to be. This is where you will start burrowing the hole into the cup and it must be this wide.

5. With the dremel, burrow the middle of this cup to get the hollow part that will hold the content of the cup. Be careful as you do this so that you do not end up taking away a lot of the cup. Also, make sure that you leave enough space between the bottom of the hole you are creating and the bottom of the cup. This will make sure that your cup lasts well enough and does not start leaking in a while. If you do not have the machine, you can manually carry out this step but know that it will demand more time and patience.

6. After creating the hollow of the cup, smoothen what you have done with sandpaper. This will further enhance the cup's looks and make sure that the rough edges are dealt with. After this, use some oil finishing of your choice to wrap up the deal. Preferably, you may want to use walnut

oil because it offers the wood some waterproof protection that helps the cup last for much longer. You have a complete cup at this stage.

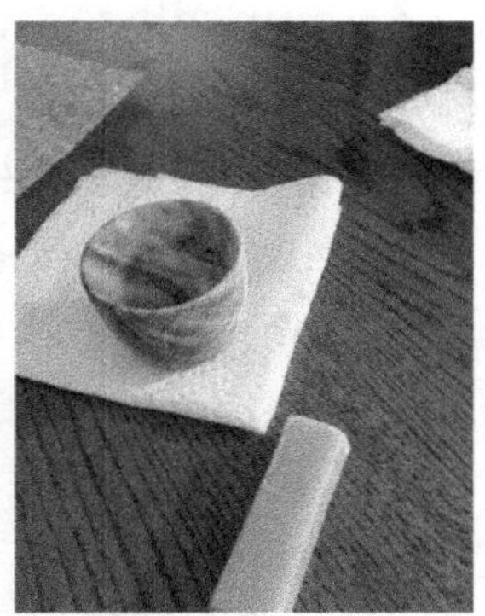

Walking Stick

This is another easy project you can complete in no time. It is a great fit for beginners and you can take it a step further the more advanced you get with whittling.

Supplies needed

- A long, sturdy stick
- Carving knife
- Oil finish
- Saw

Steps

1. Find the best stick for the project at hand. Depending on the height of the person who will be using the stick, you want to make sure that you find a stick that is long enough for the person and won't break when placed under the amount of pressure it will eventually come under. You may want to use a hardwood like maple, alder, or cherry. While selecting the wood for this purpose, make sure that whatever you pick has not been infested by insects and is not riddled with holes.

2. With your saw, trim the stick you have gotten to the length you need for the project you are working on. To be sure of the length, stand straight and plant the stick on the ground as you would when you are walking.

3. Whittle off the bark of the stick you are using. However, you can choose to skip this step if you feel the bark makes the stick look better and if it is smooth enough. To do this, make use of the cutting knife that you have. For the best of results, use short and shallow push strokes to get this done.

4. When you have removed the bark of the stick, allow the walking stick to dry. There is every tendency that the part of the stick you just exposed will be a bit wet. To make sure that you get the most out of your project, allow it to dry.

5. Add creative touches to the stick that has dried. You may consider carving your initials to the stick with the knife you have for simpler decorations, or you can carve a spiral groove at the top of the stick. This will help make the stick easier for you to grab on to.

6. With your sandpaper, rub all over the stick to make it smooth and better to look at. When you are done, apply the oil finish on the stick and allow it to dry off.

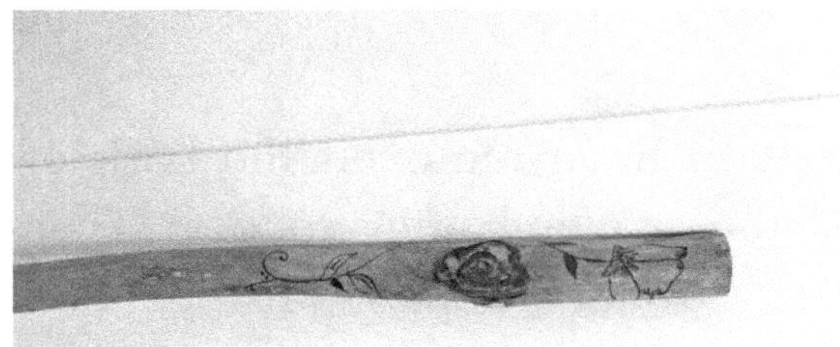

Wooden Dog

Supplies needed

- Wood
- Carving knife
- Oil finish
- Saw
- Protective gear
- Printing paper (cardboard or any other paper that can be used for printing)

Steps

Before you begin with trying to create a dog out of wood, you must remember to take it slowly and flexibly as whittling is a task of meditation and relaxation. Trying to rush through the project could result in getting yourself harmed, and it can also ruin the project at hand. These are the general steps to follow;

1. Plan and draw out the model. This is the first step in the dog whittling process. Decide on the breed of the dog you want to carve, draw it out on the printing paper with the necessary details on the model you are drawing. Conversely, if you are not much of an artist and feel better with taking a photo with a camera, you may want to stick to that choice. The idea is to have a miniature representation of the dog you are looking to carve out. As a tip, try making the first model with clay. This will help bring a lot of things into focus as you work your way through.

2. Carve the model you have drawn on the block of wood you are using for the project and begin by cutting out the first wood blank shaped like the dog. To achieve this, transfer the outline you created in step A to the wooden block using a pencil. Try as much as you can to make accurate measurements while you work on this stage

because this will determine a lot with regards to how the final project will look.

3. With as much precision as you can, begin to carve out the outline you have transferred to the wood. Just the same way you worked on carving out the spoon from the wood block, use the same idea for this step. You should begin with the face of the dog and add in as many details as you can while you proceed.

4. For the best results, you should clamp the wood to a table. It will leave both your hands free so you can have a better grip on the wooden piece you are carving.

5. Pay attention to allowing your dog to get as many details as possible at this stage. To achieve this, you may have to carve in all known directions to make it look lifelike.

6. When you are done with the stage above, smoothen rough edges with sandpaper. This will

make sure that your work looks clean and that you can continue without feeling uncomfortable.

7. Add the final touches to the dog and that will be all. The final touches include further whittling where it is needed, cleaning the piece with sandpaper, and finally, using the oil finish to make sure that what you have is as clean as it can get.

You should have something of this nature when you are done;

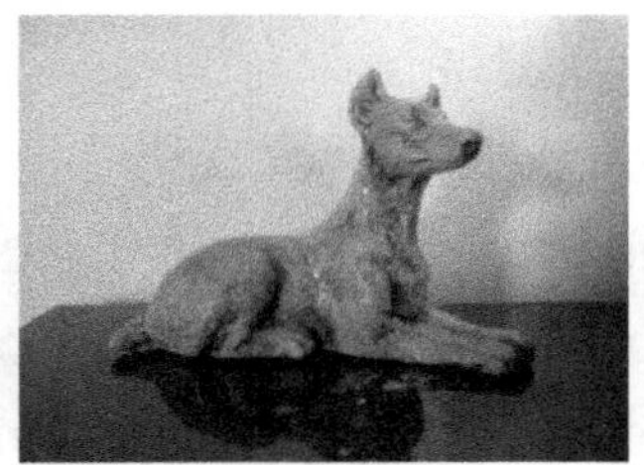

Wooden Cat

This is another wooden project you can embark upon at any time if you have all the materials that are needed. As a matter of fact, carving a cat is relatively easier than carving other animals because cats have a minimalist body structure.

Supplies needed

- An illustrated sample of the cat printed on paper
- Wood block
- Carving knife
- Protective gear
- Clamps and a vise

Steps

1. The steps to creating your cat are similar to the steps involved in carving a dog. The first thing you need to do is create an outline of the cat you want to carve on a wooden block.

2. Mark stop cuts on the wooden block where you have transferred the outline of the cat. To achieve this, use a chip knife and make stop cuts on the cat's neck, face, legs, and tail. Stop cuts guide your carving process and make sure that you carve the right kind of cat you're looking to.

3. With your carving knife (and maybe chisel), begin to chip the wooden block. Following the outline that you have created, carve out the

excesses from the wooden block. When you do this well, you should be left with a rough figure of the cat you are working on.

4. Clean out the rough edges with sandpaper. With a smaller carving knife, make sure that you carve until you get to the outline you drew. This way, you do not leave anything untouched. When you have done this, clean out the cat once again with sandpaper, and finish off with oil.

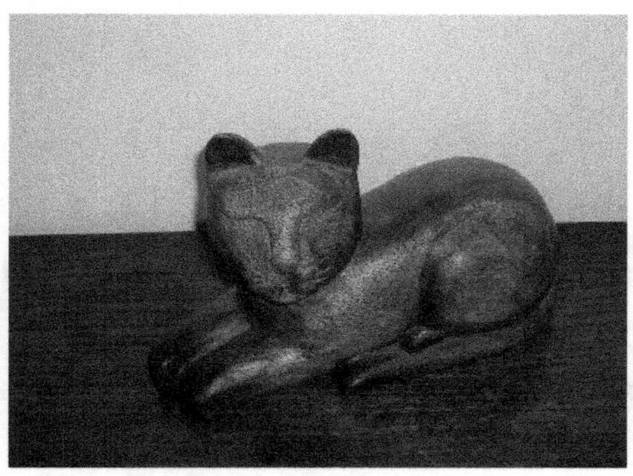

Wooden Elephant

Supplies needed

- A block of wood
- Elephant outline
- Carving knife
- Sandpaper
- Protective gear
- Oil finish
- Chisel

Steps

1. Select the best kind of wood for the project. This will require some more carving than the last two projects, so you need to make sure that you have wood that won't frustrate you while at it.

2. Transfer the elephant's outline on the wooden block and start the process by cutting out the excesses from the wooden block. Leave some space between the size of the printed outline and

the wood cutting you will make. This space will be accounted for much later on.

3. When you have outlined the whole elephant on wood, start the whittling process from the head. Following the wood grain direction, trace the outline of the elephant head using your carving knife and chisel if you need to. With stop cuts, highlight the nose, trunks, and distinct features of the elephant's face. Also, pay attention to the elephant's trunk and make sure to outline it with your carving knife as you work on the face. The trunk's shape should be consistent with the shape from the outline you printed on the block of wood.

4. Define the ears of the elephant. Once you are done with the face, begin to work on the ears of the elephant. It would be best if you held the piece of wood with a clamp while you work on this so that you have extra space to work with your hands. With your carving knife, make stop cuts toward the bottom of the ears and carefully begin to carve them out. Remember that it is safer

to use push strokes for this carving not to wound yourself.

5. Work on the rest of the body. Carve, chip, and sandpaper as you go along. This will ensure that you create an elephant that is just the same as the one you transferred from the outline.

6. Put finishing touches and use the oil finish to enhance the looks of the elephant once you are done. You can decide to spice things up a bit by making some drawings on the elephant. It is your call.

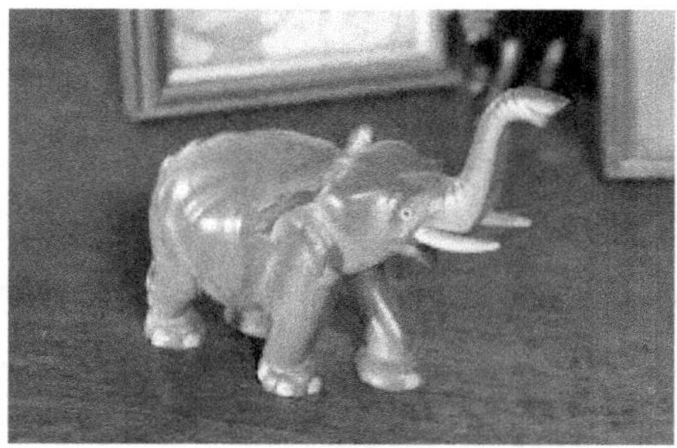

Wooden Flower

Supplies needed

- Wooden block
- Carving knife
- Oil finish
- Sandpaper
- Protective gear
- Chisel

Step

1. Select a thin wooden block that you will use for your project. For this kind of project, you want to make use of a wooden block that is soft, preferably basswood.

2. In the center of the wooden block, make a circle. You can do this with the pair of compasses that come with a mathematical set. Consider the size of the flower you want to create and the size of its petals before you get started with this part of the project. This will help you make the right choice for the size of the circle to use.

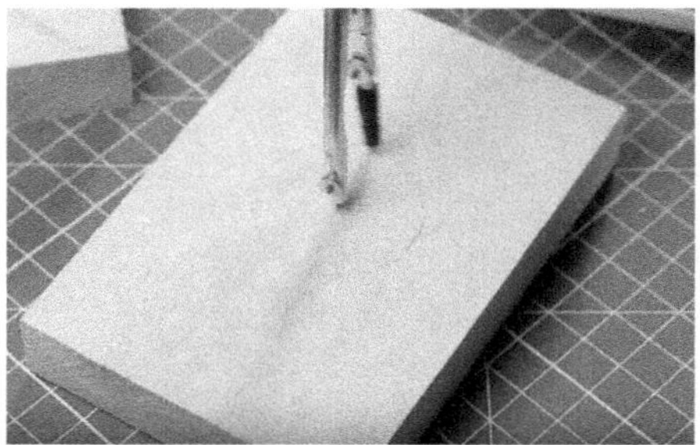

3. Outline the petals of the flower with the help of the chisel you have with you. Be careful not to ruin the flower while at it.

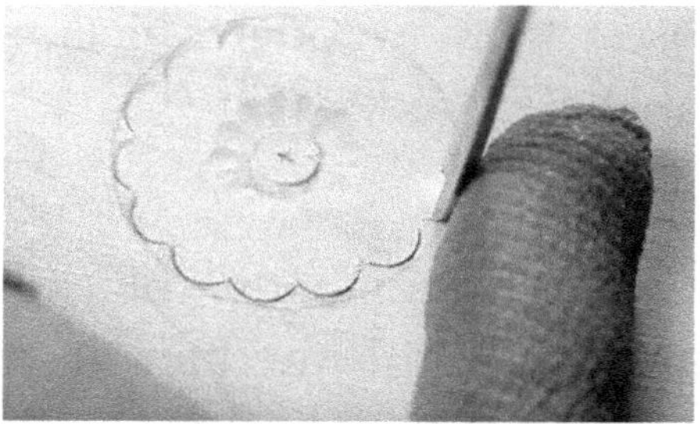

4. With the chisel, further shape the petals of the flower to make them a bit deeper. Remember to be as careful as you can be right here so that you do not take off the flowers or ruin the whole wooden block.

5. Create a few leaves for your flower. The easiest way to do this is by drawing on the wooden block with a pencil. Conversely, you can choose to chisel your way through this step. To get the most out of this step, take a look at some flowers and let their looks spark your creativity. You can choose to place how many leaves you want, and you can also choose the size of the leaves you want to be in your flower.

6. Dig out some space in the spots you have drawn the leaves. This will help your flower look better. You should do this with your chisel. Also, map out the edges of the leaves and make sure that you do your best to stay within the confines of safety so as not to ruin what you have created so far. This step will bring the leaves to life and the flower will begin to take shape.

7. Go over the flower you have created and make sure that you have what you were looking to create from the start. For some more definition in the flower, smooth over the edges with sandpaper, use some colors to bring it to life, and

when the colors have dried up, apply some oil finish to it. The oil finish will make sure that your flower lasts for much longer, and it will help the colors you have painted on the wood to stand out.

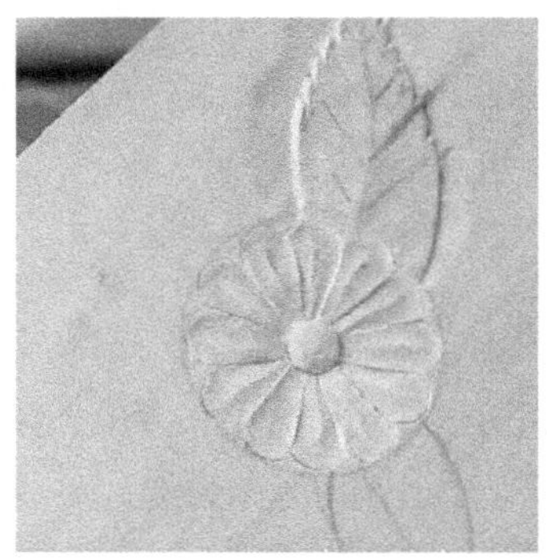

Natural Elbow Boomerang

This is a simple boomerang that can be created by anyone at any time, with the right resources.

Supplies needed

- Pocket saw
- Grafting wax
- Glue
- Sandpaper
- Safety gear
- Carving knife

- Oil finish

Steps

1. Find the appropriate piece of wood that can be used for this project. For starters, it is recommended that you search this out yourself. You can take a walk into the forest and seek for a piece of wood that looks like an elbow boomerang.

2. When you find the right piece of wood, cut it out from the tree. Whittle out the bark of this piece of wood, and let it dry. The right piece of wood should look like this.

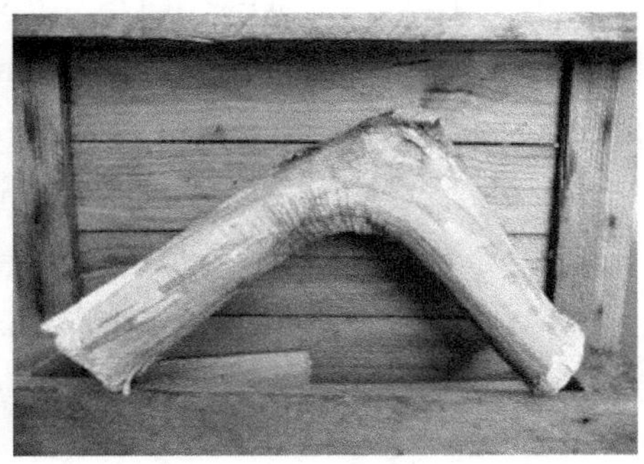

3. After the elbow has dried, prepare it by planing it to have a flat surface on both sides. This will involve a bit of maneuvering on both sides of the wood with a plane or sander. When you have achieved the plane shape, saw the wood into smaller and flatter boomerangs. You should have something like this at this point.

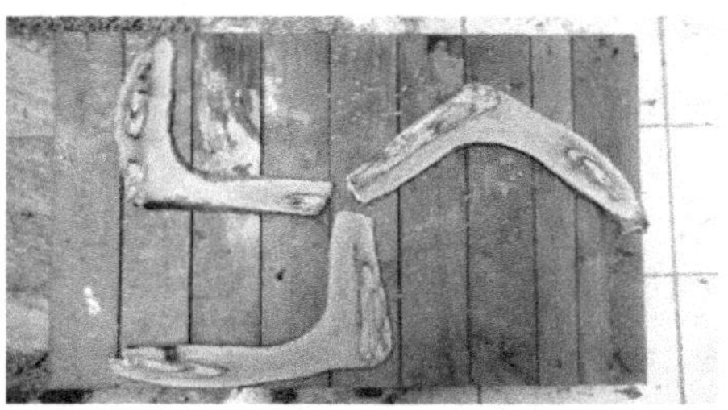

4. Design the boomerang that you want to work with. You do not need to do a lot of thinking at this stage. Just take a close look at what the tree has presented you with and make the most out of the wood's natural design. This could be to further make marks like your initials on the boomerang, or do whatever comes to mind. The aim here is to get creative and not have to follow any set down template.

5. Carve out the edges so that they are slightly curved and look less jagged. You can make use of a smoothening machine or the sander you have been working with.

6. When you are done with the last step, you can further customize the boomerang. To achieve this, you can choose to paint the boomerang you're your desired colors, and when the paint dries up, oil it with the oil finish you kept aside. You should have something that looks like this

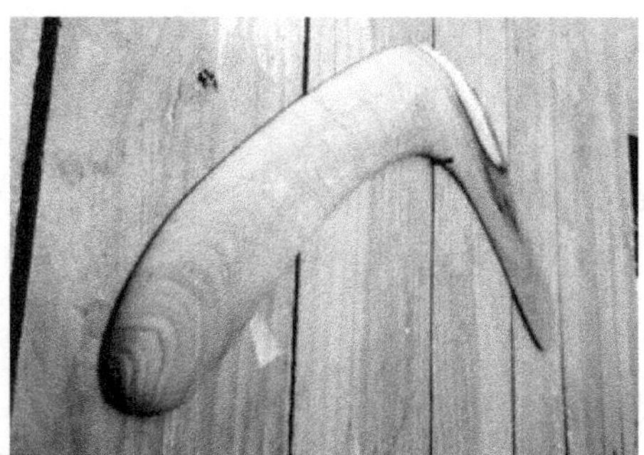

Spiral Pencil

This is a super easy project, but it requires a lot of time and carefulness to pull off.

Supplies needed

- Wooden pencil
- Carving knife
- Oil finish

Steps

1. Select the right pencil to use for your project. We
   pointed out earlier that although this is an easy
   project, you need a lot of patience to pull it off
   because if you try to rush through it, you may
   end up spoiling the pencil you are looking to
   create.

2. After selecting the pencil you want to use, draw
   two lines that go all the way around the pencil in
   a spiral shape. You want to make sure that these
   lines are parallel and do not make a mistake with
   the spacing. The space between these lines must
   be the same all around the pencil.

3. When you have completed step two, cut out the
   lines you have drawn around the pencil. Be
   careful to follow the lines you have drawn and

make sure that you do not cut too hard that you snap the pencil in two.

4. With your carving knife, clean out the pencil well enough so that what you have cut does not look rough. To further make things look good, use a small piece of sandpaper to clean out the rest of the pencil.

5. Oil with the finish you have and allow the pencil to dry. For the best results, use a rounded pencil for this project (especially if you are a beginner). If you are advanced, you can give a six-sided pencil a try. You should have something like this at this point.

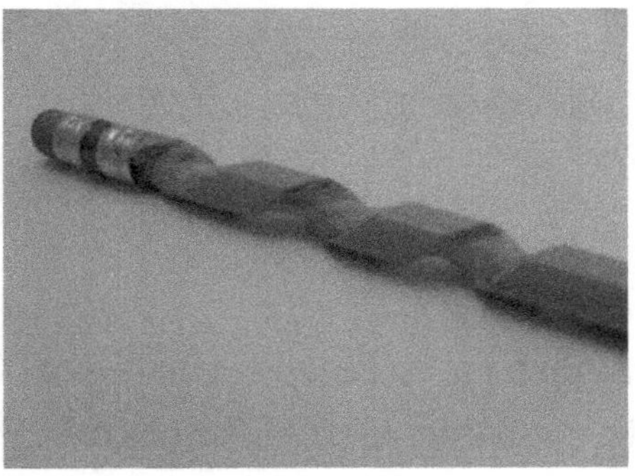

Wooden Knives

You may be surprised at this one because you may have known knives to be metallic alone. However, with the right knowledge, materials, and skills, you can create a wooden knife. Although they may not be as sharp as the metallic knives, wooden knives are super cool and useful when you come to think of it.

Supplies needed

- Wood
- Knife
- Protective gear
- Twine or thin rope. However, if these are not readily available, you can do without them.
- Oil finish
- Sandpaper or sharpening apparatus

Steps

1. First, choose a suitable piece of wood. While doing this, make sure that you put the wood piece's thickness and strength into consideration.

You do not want to use a wood piece that will snap in two in no time, neither do you want to select a piece that will be too difficult for you to fashion into a knife.

2. Select one end of the wooden stick that you have selected for use. Sharpen one of the ends of this stick. This will be the tip of the wooden blade. Do this after the fashion of how knife blades look. For the best of results, use the push stroke to achieve this, and be sure to keep your hands out of the way.

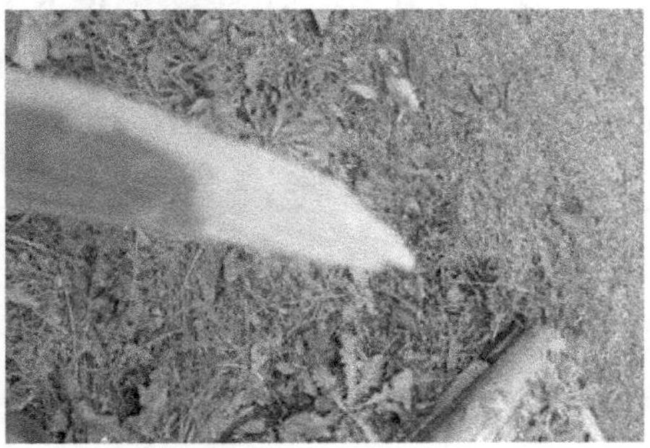

3. Define the handle of the knife by making a groove toward the other end of the stick you are carving. This groove will separate the knife's handle from the rest of the knife, which will be

the blade. You should have something of this nature when you are done with this step.

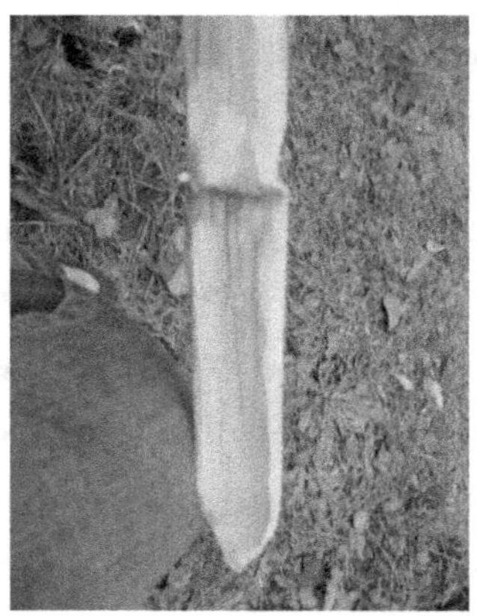

4. Get creative with the handle you have differentiated from the rest of the knife. Whatever you can do to make it beautiful and more alluring to the sight should be done at this point. Make patterns with your carving knife, carve your name on it; the idea is to make sure that the knife is not as bland-looking as it would be if you do otherwise.

5. With your sandpaper (or whatever will do the job of sharpening for you), begin to work on sharpening the blade of the knife you are creating. Chip away at the wood in such a way

that the blade gets smaller and sharper than it was. When you think it has become as sharp as it can be, you can stop this process. However, note that you should be on the lookout for when the knife will become as sharp as it can get. This is wood and not metal. Do not expect that it will be as sharp as a metal blade.

6. Use the oil finish to make it appear better, and paint if you would want to. Be careful to know that what you have created is quite sharp and not something you should treat like a toy, especially if you have minors around you.

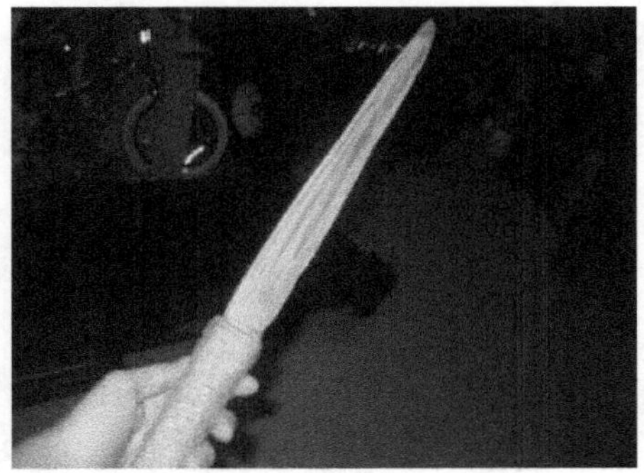

Wooden Gnome

This is a fun project that you can create from a piece of salvaged wood. Although it can be completed in record time, you need some amount of skillfulness to pull this one off because you need to pay attention to the details on the wood and carve carefully. You also need to have some basic knowledge of painting and color combinations for the best effects.

Supplies needed

- A piece of salvaged wood.
- Carving knife
- Some paint of different colors
- Oil finish
- Sandpaper
- Protective gear
- Jigsaw puzzle pieces

Steps

1. The first step you must take if you want to be successful with this project is to ensure that you have selected the right piece of wood for your project. The right piece of wood is dependent on your skill level. For a beginner, you may want to

go for something softer and easier to carve so that you do not have to spend the whole day on this project. If you are at the intermediate level of carving, you may want to try out something firmer, which may last for a longer time.

2. Cut out a wooden bar or a block from the wooden piece you have. This is where you will make an imprint of the gnome you are carving and cut it out. For this step, it is pertinent that you get the shape well because the shape is largely responsible for how your gnome will turn out.

3. To make the gnome's imprint you will carve out, you can follow either of two modes. You can choose to;

i. Take a picture of a miniature gnome, imprint it on the wooden block, and then cut out from there.

ii. On the other hand, you can use the jigsaw pieces from the list of things you need to carry out this exercise. For this project, we will be making use of this style.

4. Place your wood in a vice grip and make the wood's desired pattern with the jigsaw pieces. Pay attention and make sure that the pattern you are making looks like the attached picture. This is because you want the gnome to look like it should.

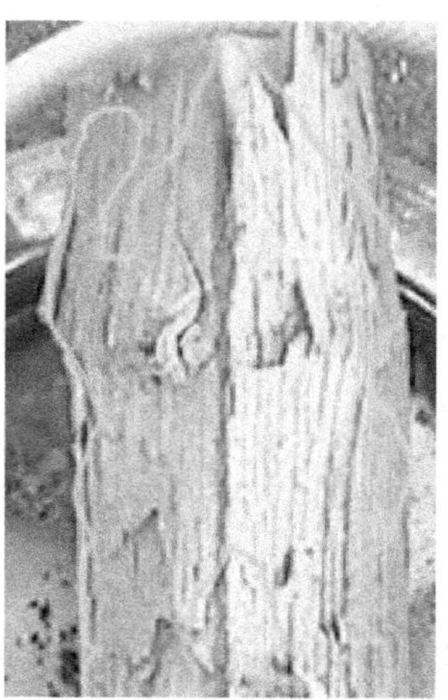

5. From the outline you have on the piece of wood, start cutting out the gnome. You will have to cut, smoothen, cut again, and keep at it until you have gotten the flat shape of the gnome you are

working on. This will take some time and skills to complete, but remember to refer to the picture of the gnome you are trying to model so that you do not veer off the model.

6. Keep up with the step above till you have something of this nature (if you are using the same template as discussed in this project).

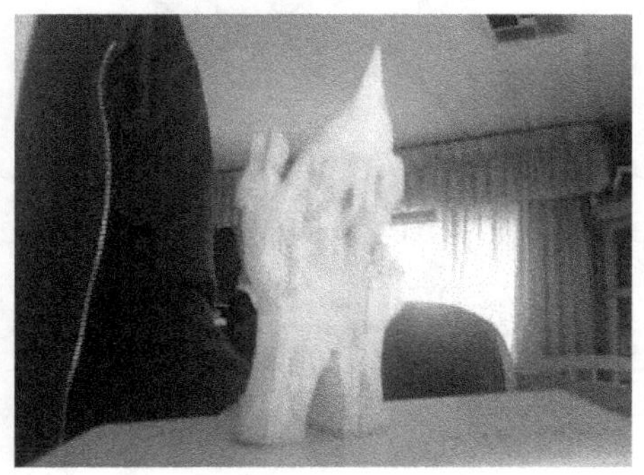

7. When you have gotten to this stage, you will need to bring your knowledge of painting to bear. This is where you get creative with the whole process. Mix different colors for different parts of the gnome to get the best effects. You can mix acrylic base paints and switch up the shades of colors to expand your creative options for the best of results. The picture attached should be used as

inspiration, and that is what your gnome should look like when you are done.

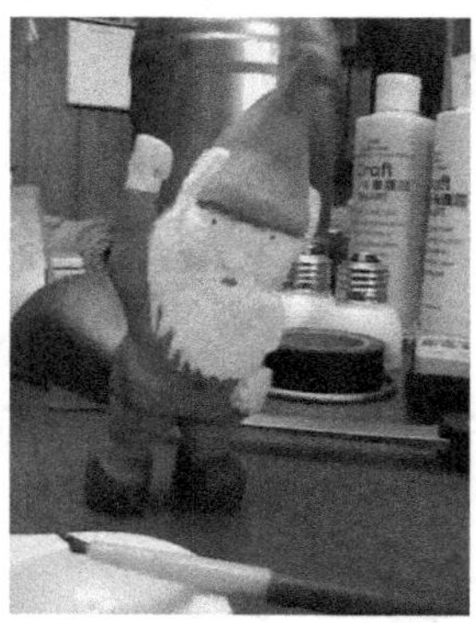

8. Do not forget to put finishing touches to the gnome when you are done with the painting and dried. Apply some oil finish to the gnome as this will help it last for longer and improve the lustre of the final output.

Wooden Rainsticks

This is another fun project you can embark upon at any time. It is relatively easy to create, but you will need to follow the details captured below if you want to be successful at it.

First off, rainsticks are long, hollow tubes filled with small pebbles or beans and have small pins or thorns arranged carefully inside it. When the stick is turned or rattled, the pebbles or beans fall to the other side of the stick, making a sound that can be likened to the sound of falling rain. Over the last 200 years, these have become quite popular and tourists usually trip for them when they go on vacation in places where rainsticks are sold. This is a project you definitely want to try your hands on and it is suitable for you if you have some working knowledge of whittling and how it works.

Supplies needed

- Some pieces boards from a window blind
- Protective gear
- Oil finish
- Pebbles or the beans

Steps

1. For this project, you will need six boards out of the window blind you are using. You can decide to leave the boards as long as they are or to cut

them in half - depending on how long you want the stick to be after you are done.

2. Lay out these boards on a table and arrange them side by side. As the need arises, you may have to make certain cuts at 30-degree angles at the sides of the board so that they can lap well against each other. At the end of this project, you will have a hexagonal shape, so you need to ensure that the boards are at an angle where they can easily overlap.

3. When you have made sure that the boards, when assembled, will give you the hexagonal shape you are looking for, it is time to assemble them with masking tape. Lay them out against a table and tape them together. While doing this, make sure that the boards' surfaces are clean so that the tape can adhere strongly to the boards. This should be the project at this point.

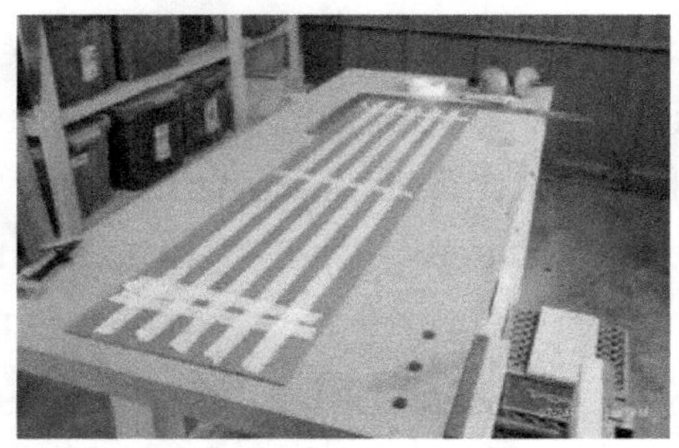

4. Turn over the assembly to the other side and fill the spaces on the boards with glue. This should make them tight and less likely to fall apart. When you have closed the tubes, glue them further with masking tape. Be careful to tape the places that you previously filled with glue. This will make sure that your stick has a good look, and it will further reinforce the strength of the glue you applied in the last step.

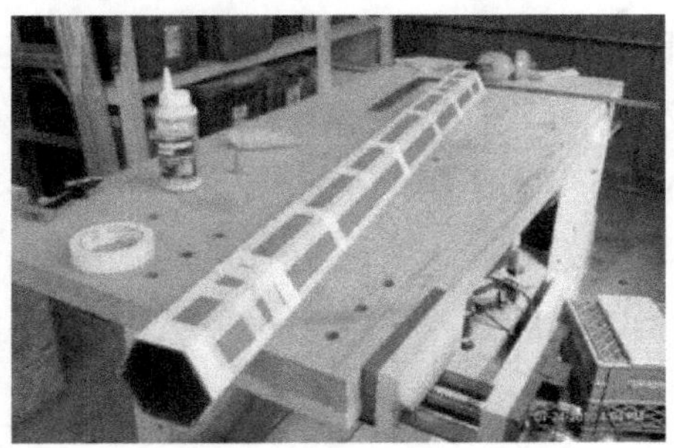

5. Place the end of the tube you have created so far on a piece of wood and outline the wood piece that will form the stick's end. When you have cut out the end pieces, drill a hole in the center of these pieces. Be careful when you are doing this. You do not want to pierce the whole piece through, so you should stop piercing when you are about 3/4 ways through.

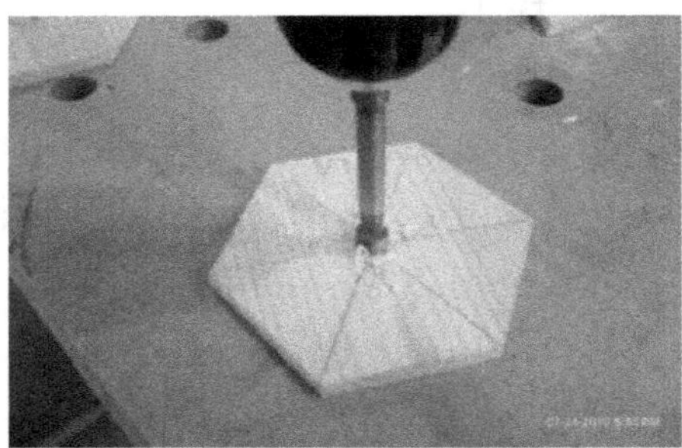

6. You are going to create a wooden dowel at this point. The dowel must be the tube's length, plus twice (2 ends) the depth of the holes you made on both end caps. Glue one of the ends you created to one side of the wooden dowel. This you will fit on one end of the hexagon you created earlier

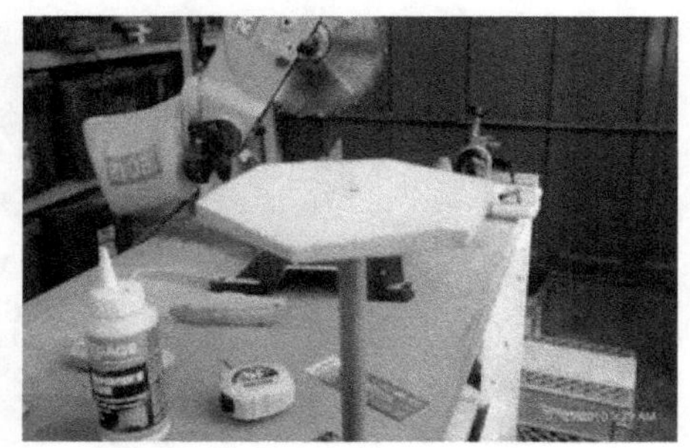

7. Set out what you have created and allow it to dry. While this happens, begin to cut out the expanded metal lath baffles. These are metal, mesh-shaped, rounded materials that you will fit into the stick to ensure that you have what you are looking to create at the end of the project. Depending on the size of the stick you are creating and the patience you have, cut these. Note that the more you can make, the better your project will be once you are done.

This is what they look like.

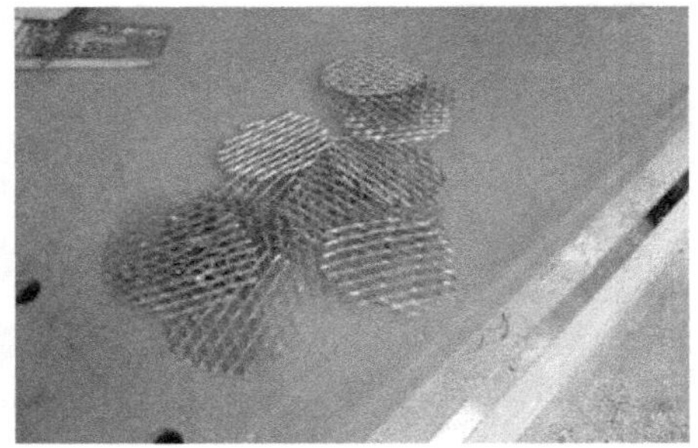

8. Glue all the baffles you have created to the dowel using some glue from a glue gun. Be sure that there is just the right amount of space between the baffles while you do this. This is what it would look like once you are done.

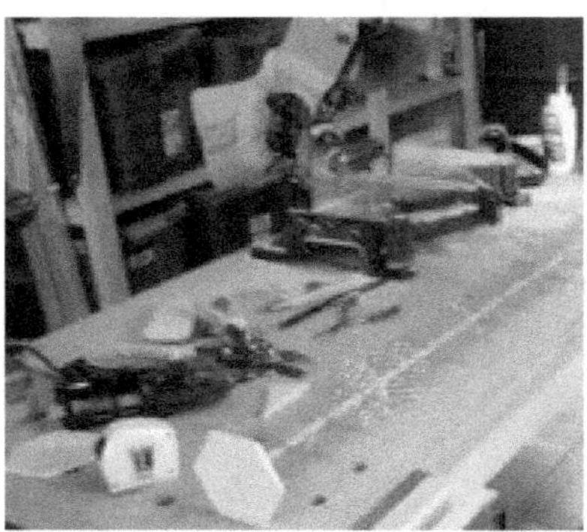

9. Slip the dowel you assembled into the stick and glue one of the ends in place. Allow this to dry for at least one hour. When it is dry, put the pebbles you have into the stick and glue the other cover. Conversely, you can use some rice or anything of that nature that can produce sound in the stick. Make sure that you use something that is small enough to fall through the meshes of the baffles. When you are done, finish off with oil, paint, and allow the stick to dry.

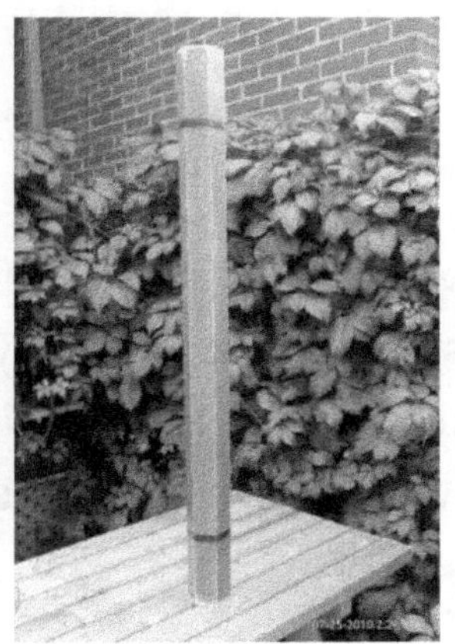

Carved Viking Chess Piece

Supplies needed

- Piece of wood
- Saw
- Carving knife
- Sandpaper or whatever you will need for smoothening the wood as you work
- Oil finish

Steps

1. Select the best wood for the project at hand. Keep in mind your progress level as you do this not to pick a piece of wood that will end up being too hard for you to work around.

2. Break the wood into shape. Depending on the shape and size of the wood you got, you may have to break it again and again. For this project, you need a wooden piece that is shaped like those in the picture.

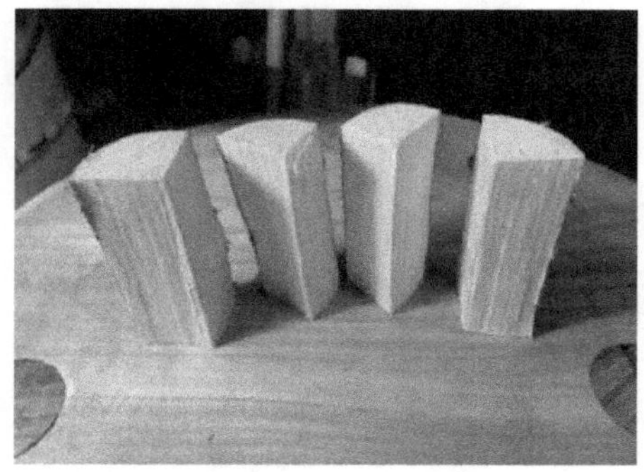

3. With your carving knife, whittle off the bark of the wood you are using for the project. You may also want to smoothen things a bit with some sandpaper at this point, or you may skip it if you do not want to.

4. This is where you start the work. With your carving knife, get to work carving the details of the face. To make things a bit easier for yourself, you may want to try using a little, round plastic as the eyes of the chess piece you are creating. Stick this in the right positions with glue if you do. On the other hand, you can carefully carve out the details by whittling off at the right places. Here's a picture for you to draw inspiration from.

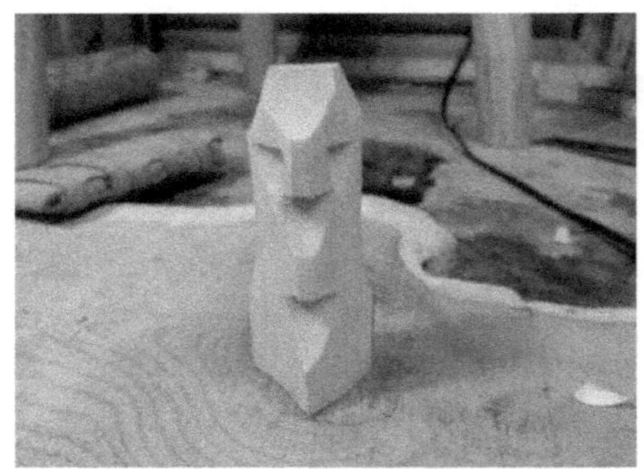

5. Add finishing touches to the chess piece. Whittle out the finer details, smoothen with sandpaper and cover with an oil finish for the best effects.

Hand Carved Pizza Wheel

Supplies needed

- Stainless spoon
- Wood piece
- 1 inch screw
- Drill
- Masking tape
- Punzon
- Hammer
- Machete

- Cutter
- Oil finish/varnish
- Beeswax
- Compasses from a mathematical set

Steps

1. Wrap the bowl of the stainless spoon with some leather and smash it with an anvil. This step aims to reduce the curvature of the spoon and make it suitable for your needs. If you were to use a hammer for this step, you would most likely dent the spoon and it won't be suitable for your needs.

2. With the help of the math compass you have with you, find the center of the spoon's bowl and from there, make a circle across the circumference of the bow. Puncture the middle of this circle by drilling through it, then punch the entire circle with the steel puncher.

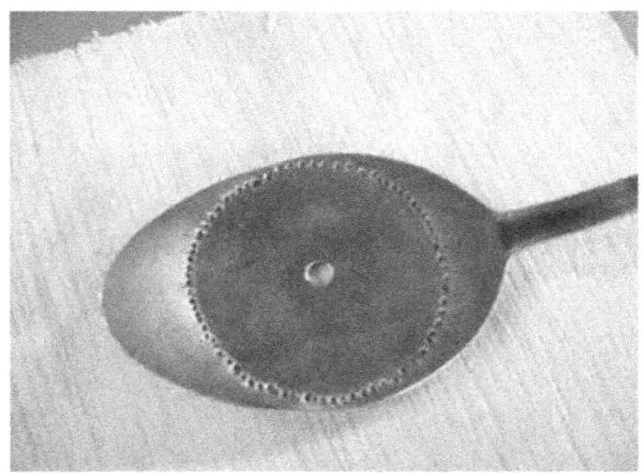

3. With the aid of the pliers, remove the remaining part of the spoon so that you are left with something of this nature.

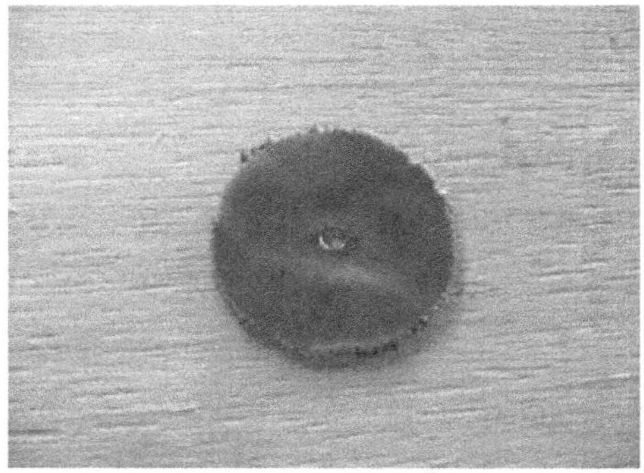

4. On a suitable piece of wood, outline the handle of what you are creating and begin to carve out this handle. Go through the motions of carving out the handle following the outline that you have created. With sandpaper, make sure that what

you have created is as smooth as possible and polish accordingly.

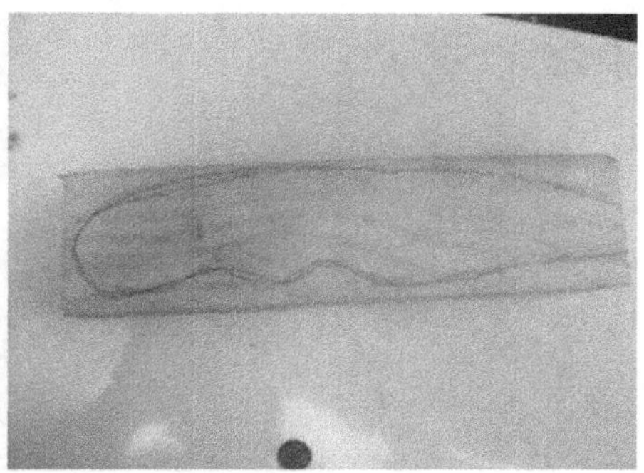

5. Go on to make the handle appear just the way you want it to be as you keep working at it.

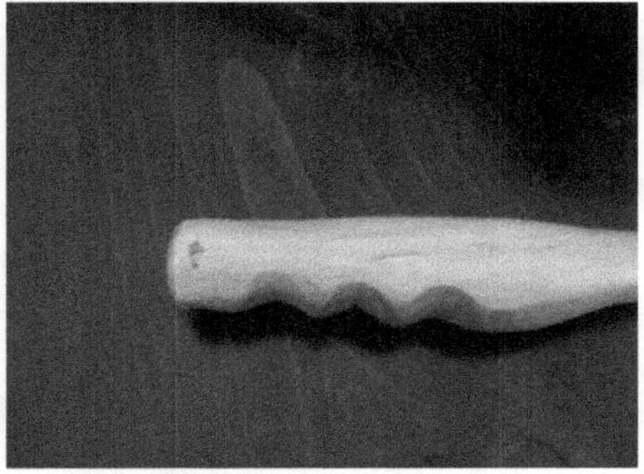

6. Fix the wheel you created to the smaller end of the handle and put finishing touches to the

project. That's it. You are done. You should have something of this nature.

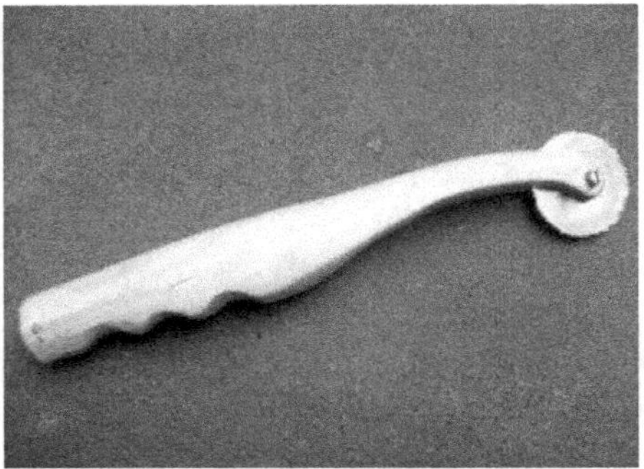

Wooden Pipe

Supplies needed

- A piece of wood (approx 1 inch square by 4 inches).
- Sandpaper and belt sander.
- Natural oils for finishing.
- 3/4 inch forstner bit, and faucet screen.
- Saw.

Steps

1. Bore the bowl of the pipe. To achieve this, make use of the Forstner bit you have, but make sure that the hole you are creating is not too deep that you cannot connect it to the other side of the pipe. Be sure to situate the Forstner bit in the middle of the wood piece you are using so that the hole that will come out will be equally spaced out on either side.

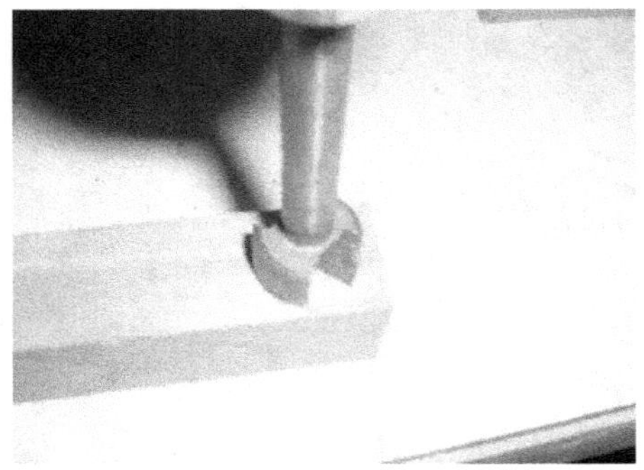

2. Bore the stem hole using a driller. While drilling, make sure the hole is situated at a point that it is at the center of the short side of the wooden bar that you are using for the pipe.

3. Connect the stem hole to the side of the bowl you bored in step one of this project. This is where the fumes from the tobacco will come out from.

4. Now that you have bored the necessary holes, it is time for you to shape the pipe. Start by cutting off the excess wood on all sides of the pipe, then shape this using the carving knife you have with you.

5. Further add definition to the pipe you are working on. Round off the square pipe with the sandpaper you have, and make sure that it is continuous with the wood from the bowl of the pipe. This should be simple as you begin to smoothen.

6. If there are other details you would like to add, feel free to add them to the project at hand. For some inspiration, you may want to add grooves to the sides of the bowl, add a little definition to the side of the stem, and make sure that your pipe is as smooth as it can be. Finish off by using a little oil finish for the pipe and you are done. You should have something of this nature.

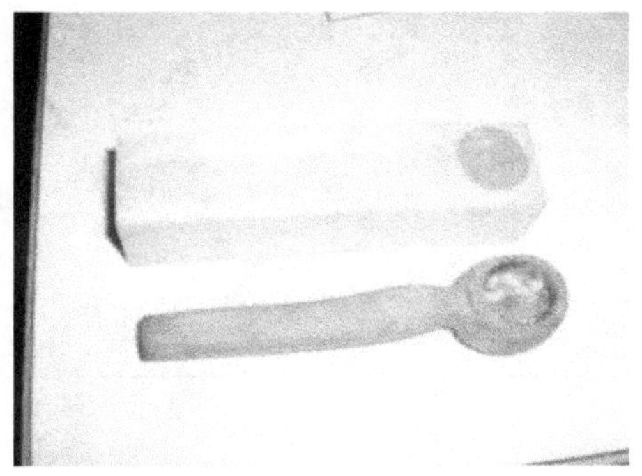

<u>**The end... almost!**</u>

Hey! We've made it to the final chapter of this book, and I hope you've enjoyed it so far.

If you have not done so yet, I would be incredibly thankful if you could take just a minute to leave a quick review on Amazon

Reviews are not easy to come by, and as an independent author with a little marketing budget, I rely on you, my readers, to leave a short review on Amazon.

Even if it is just a sentence or two!

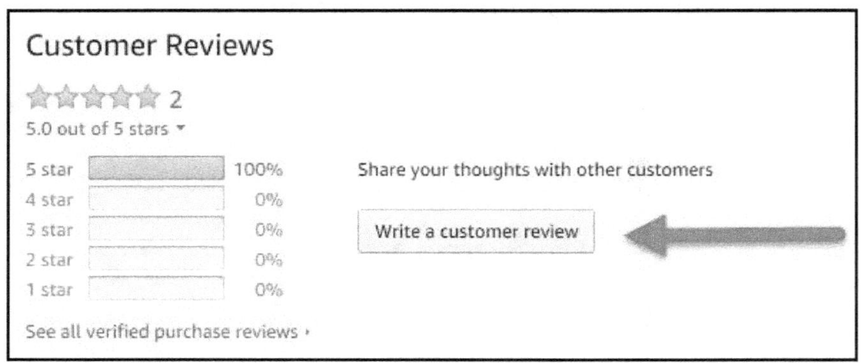

So if you really enjoyed this book, please...

\>\> Click here to leave a brief review on Amazon.

I truly appreciate your effort to leave your review, as it truly makes a huge difference.

Chapter 6

Whittling Frequently Asked Questions

1. What is the best type of wood to use for my projects?

Answer; there is really no "best" wood to use for whittling. The kind of wood you use is dependent on a few factors, including;

A. The type of project you have at hand
B. Your progress level in whittling; if you are a newbie whittler, you may want to go for softer woods so that you can carve them easily.
C. Your discretion.

Bring all these to bear when next you are embarking on a project, and select the best wood for the project you want to work on.

2. Is it necessary for me to use gloves while whittling? I find that it can be inconveniencing at times.

Answer; while you don't need to wear gloves while whittling, it is important and advisable for you to do so - especially if you are a newbie whittler. This is because it helps you keep your hands safe. Your hands will tend to come in the way of the knife while you work, so to be on the safe side, protect them.

3. What is the best wood carving method to adopt for my whittling projects?

Answer; just like the answer to the first question, there is no right or wrong way to work your way around this. The method you adopt depends on the project you are working on and your safety/convenience. However, when in doubt, you may want to find a way to make use of the push stroke.

4. What is the best whittling knife to use as a beginner?

Answer; there is no one best whittling knife for you as a beginner. All the whittling knives in the market have their advantages, disadvantages, and their strong points. All you should do is take a close look at your options and, according to your needs, make an informed decision as to what knife to settle for or to leave. You are the one that has to make the choice for yourself.

However, take a look at the following choices;

A. The Morakniv Brand and their knives
B. The Flexcut brand and their knives.

From these, you should be able to choose which is the best for you.

5. Is it okay to buy any knife I see for whittling?

Answer; no, it is not okay. Your knife will tell a lot about the success or failure of your whittling exercises. As a result, pay attention to the kind of knife you purchase. In addition to all that was pointed out in the last answer, green signs show that a knife will be a great option for you to purchase. These are detailed in the beginning section of this book. They are the things you must look out for before purchasing a knife. Find them, and make the most out of them.

6. What knife safety tips should I adopt?

Answer;

A. Be sure to use a whittling glove as you embark upon projects.
B. Return your knife to its blade lock when you are not using the knife.
C. Do not try to cut with a dirty or blunt blade.

Many other safety tips exist. Please adhere to all of them.

7. What tools do I need for a successful whittling project?

<u>Answer</u>; You need many tools to pull off your whittling projects, but generally, these are the ones you need.

A. Whittling knives
B. Sandpaper
C. Oil finishing
D. Protective gear

Conclusion

Whittling is both a great pastime and an easy way to create a lot of fun projects that you can draw upon at any time. Depending on how good you are with the skill, you can create projects that can be monetized and serve as a stream of extra income.

The options available for you are numerous. You can start with the simpler projects and scale up as you go. What's more, you can even get anyone to fall in love with the craft so that you can have your whittling allies.